MW01615310

# A Misplaced

# Mystery

## Understanding the One God

by Landon Davis

# Copyright Information

A Misplaced Mystery
Copyright © 2015 by Landon Davis

Scripture taken from the New King James Version®. Copyright © 1982 by Thomas Nelson. Used by permission. All rights reserved.

THE HOLY BIBLE, NEW INTERNATIONAL VERSION®, NIV® Copyright © 1973, 1978, 1984, 2011 by Biblica, Inc.® Used by permission. All rights reserved worldwide.

Scripture quotations marked (NLT) are taken from the Holy Bible, New Living Translation, copyright © 1996, 2004, 2007 by Tyndale House Foundation. Used by permission of Tyndale House Publishers, Inc., Carol Stream, Illinois 60188. All rights reserved.

Scripture quotations marked (NLV) are taken from the Holy Bible, New Life Version. © Christian Literature International

Christian Literature International (CLI) is a non-profit ministry dedicated to publishing and

# Copyright Information

providing the Word of God in a form that can be read and understood by new readers and the well-educated alike... and at an affordable price. We invite you to learn how the NEW LIFE Version unlocks the treasures of God's Word!

# Table of Contents

# Table of Contents

# Acknowledgements

This book is dedicated to my wife, Keri, and our children, Cale, Jude, and Lincoln.

Special thanks to our families. I'm blessed to have an amazing immediate and extended family as well as wonderful in-laws. We don't express it enough, but Keri and I are thankful for our Christian heritage. The godly environments in which we were raised were instrumental in developing our relationships with the Lord. The passion that my family exhibited for God was instilled in me and motivated me to write this book. A passion for His kingdom helped my wife to be patient with me as I studied, wrote, and endlessly bounced ideas off of her.

I want to honor the pastors and ministers in my life. First and foremost my dad, Rev. Steve Davis; without him, I would be lost. He has been my example, teacher, pastor, father, and friend. I'm also thankful for the influences of Pastor Tom Singles, Pastor David Gilmer, Pastor Lawrence Buller, Rev. Anthony Howell, Rev. Harry Powell,

# Acknowledgements

Rev. Rocky Morehead, and my big brother, Rev. Chad Davis.

I must recognize the saints of Van Buren United Pentecostal Church and Marianna First United Pentecostal Church for loving me and allowing me to preach. Much of the material for this book came from sermons that I preached in these pulpits.

Finally, Adam Avaritt convinced me to write this book and then stayed after me to finish. He along with Donna Parker provided invaluable assistance with editing. Thanks to both for the encouragement and the help.

To all my friends in the UPCI, particularly the great Arkansas District, I wish I could say to each of you individually, "Please buy my book."

# Introduction

This book is intended to be lay-friendly. There aren't many Greek words or theological terms. It isn't lacking in content, but the presentation is as simple as possible. It should appeal to preachers, established saints, new converts, and youth.

The material may be controversial to some, but the tone of this book is not meant to be "ugly." My intention isn't to argue. I just want to exalt Jesus according to the truth.

One thing that the reader will notice is the use of varied translations. I used the following: KJV (King James Version), NKJV (New King James Version), WEB (World English Bible), NIV (New International Version), NLT (New Living Translation), and NLV (New Life Version).

The KJV, NKJV, and WEB are more literal translations (think 'word for word') of the traditional text. The NIV, NLT, and NLV are more dynamic translations (translating the meaning of the passage as clearly as possible for the modern reader, not necessarily word for word). These are

# Introduction

based on essentially the same Greek text as the KJV although there are a few minor variations.

I understand that many churches use the KJV exclusively. In fact, I preach from the KJV myself. I prefer the more literal translations of the traditional Greek text. However, this does not mean that other translations are not valuable tools to help share the gospel.

There is biblical precedent for using various versions to present the Bible in an understandable manner. The New Testament quotes much of the Old Testament. Since the epistles were written primarily to Greeks and Hellenized Jews, we shouldn't be surprised that the Greek version of the Old Testament is usually quoted. It is important to note that this version is slightly different from the Hebrew version of the Scriptures and is not always a literal translation. For example, some ancient Hebrew expressions were written in a more dynamic fashion so that they would be understandable to the readers of that day.

# Introduction

I can't say that the learned Apostle Paul considered both versions to be of equal authenticity. We do know that the Greek version was the most accessible and understandable to the Greek speaking saints, so he used it for the glory of God to reveal Christ and salvation to those that were in darkness.

I write during an age when the majority of people are unfamiliar with the Bible and the sometimes archaic language of the KJV. With this in mind, I decided to follow the Apostolic example and use the tools available to me in making this book as accessible to as many people as possible.

If you are not comfortable with translations other than the King James, I encourage you to read this book with your Bible handy. As you come across a Scripture, look it up in the Bible you trust. You will find that I have been careful not to misconstrue the meaning of the verses. The revelation of the Mighty God in Christ will leap from the pages of your Bible.

# Introduction

I have tried to make this book as short as possible. I wish that I could include entire verses and the context surrounding them, but I have limited the quotations to the portions of the verses that are most pertinent to the material.

A few key verses are used multiple times. Usually this is not only because the verses are applicable to multiple chapters but also as a point of emphasis so that the reader will become familiar with them.

Finally, I want to encourage you to read with an open mind and an open heart. We are instructed to prove all things. I prayed many times while writing this book that God would give me understanding of His truth. I recommend that you pray a similar prayer. If it is truth, as I believe it is, God can open your eyes and your heart to receive it.

In the name of Jesus Christ,
Landon Davis

# Comparing Two Views of God

Chapter 1: Comparing Two Views of One God.

There is nothing more important than knowing God. He has revealed Himself to us in His Word. After much study, my understanding of the nature of God does not align with the traditional understanding of the Godhead.

For some, there is no need to read further. If I'm not a Trinitarian, I must be lost. In many peoples' minds, there are only two categories: Trinitarians and unbelievers. I could be a Baptist, a Methodist, a Pentecostal, and maybe even a Catholic and make it to Heaven, but if I don't believe that God exists eternally in three separate persons then I am a heretic. Doctrine seemingly makes no major difference unless you dare to avoid the unscriptural word "persons" when describing God.

If this is the definition of a heretic, then I must make the same confession as Paul.

Acts 24:14 (KJV)
"But this I confess unto thee, that after the way

# Comparing Two Views of God

which they call heresy, so worship I the God of my fathers, believing all things which are written in the law and in the prophets."

Marginalizing anyone who thinks differently and calling them names is much easier than considering their views and examining your own beliefs.

For those who are willing to look more circumspectly, this book will compare the orthodox position and what I consider the more biblical view, oftentimes called Oneness.

| |
|---|
| **Trinity:** There are three distinct persons yet in unity they are one God. The three co-equal, co-eternal persons of co-essence are God the Father, God the Son, and God the Holy Ghost. |
| **Oneness:** There is one God. He is a Spirit. He has manifested Himself to men in different ways, primarily as our Father in creation, in the Son for redemption, and as the Holy Spirit actively working, infilling, and ministering throughout the world. |

# Comparing Two Views of God

One minister described the core difference between these two belief systems this way: "Trinitarians believe in one what and three whos while Oneness adherents believe in one who and three whats." [1]

This statement is overly generalized but basically true. Is it more biblical to view the Almighty as one God that exists in three distinct persons or as one personal Spirit that we perceive in three primary ways?

I've summarized the Oneness view by quoting Scripture. The Trinitarian view is more complex and nuanced so I have copied the Athanasian Creed. This statement is generally accepted as an accurate portrayal of Trinitarian theology.

### Oneness

**1.** "In the beginning God" (Gen. 1:1).

**2.** "The LORD our God is one LORD" (Deu.6:4).

**3.** "God is a Spirit" (John 4:24).

# Comparing Two Views of God

**4.** "God was manifest in the flesh" (I Tim. 3:16).

**5.** "A son is given. His name shall be called Mighty God, the Everlasting Father" (Isa. 9:6). His name shall be called Immanuel for He is "God with us" (Matt. 1:23). His name shall be called "Jesus for he shall save his people" (Matt. 1:21). "There is none other name under heaven given among men, whereby we must be saved" (Acts 4:12).

**6.** "God was in Christ" (II Cor. 5:19). "All the fullness of the Godhead dwelleth in him bodily" (Col 2:9).

**7.** "He is the express image of His *(God's)* person" (Heb. 1:3).

**8.** He is "the only wise God our Savior" (Jude 1:25).

**9.** He has "all power in heaven and earth" (Matt. 28:18).

**10.** We are "complete in Him" (Col. 2:10).

# Comparing Two Views of God

## The Trinity: Athanasian Creed

"We worship one God in Trinity, and Trinity in Unity; neither confounding the Persons; nor dividing the Essence. For there is one Person of the Father; another of the Son; and another of the Holy Ghost. But the Godhead of the Father, of the Son, and of the Holy Ghost, is all one; the Glory equal, the Majesty co-eternal. Such as the Father is; such is the Son; and such is the Holy Ghost. The Father uncreated; the Son uncreated; and the Holy Ghost uncreated. The Father unlimited; the Son unlimited; and the Holy Ghost unlimited. The Father eternal; the Son eternal; and the Holy Ghost eternal. And yet they are not three eternals; but one eternal. As also there are not three uncreated; nor three infinites, but one uncreated; and one infinite. So likewise the Father is Almighty; the Son Almighty; and the Holy Ghost Almighty. And yet they are not three Almighties; but one Almighty. So the Father is God; the Son is God; and the Holy Ghost is God. And yet they are not three Gods; but one God. So likewise the Father is Lord; the Son Lord; and the Holy Ghost Lord. And yet not three Lords; but one Lord. For like as we are compelled by the Christian verity; to acknowledge every Person by himself to be God and Lord; so are we forbidden by the catholic religion; to say, there are three Gods, or three Lords. The Father is made of none; neither created, nor begotten. The Son is of the Father alone; not made, nor created; but begotten. The Holy Ghost is of the Father and of the Son; neither made, nor created, nor begotten; but proceeding. So there is one Father, not three Fathers; one Son, not three Sons; one Holy Ghost, not three Holy Ghosts. And in this Trinity none is before, or after another; none is greater, or less than another. But the whole three Persons are coeternal, and coequal. So that in all things, as aforesaid; the Unity in Trinity, and the Trinity in Unity, is to be worshipped."

**Chapter One Main Idea: Trinitarians believe in one God that exists in three persons. Oneness teaches that there is one God that has interacted with men and manifested Himself in various ways.**

## Chapter 2: Worshiping a Chicken

*Pete knew one thing. He would never eat chicken again. He just hoped that he could be forgiven for all his trips to Chick-fil-A. It did seem that he had found favor somehow. He was a miracle after all.*

*He would never forget his near death experience. After the accidental overdose, everything was blurry, dark, and lonely. Suddenly, a bright light shined, and he saw the Mighty Sky Chicken seated on the throne in Heaven.*

*Everyone thought that he was crazy when he shared his testimony, but he was not discouraged. In fact, their doubts provided motivation to prove his claims. He searched until he found the necessary Scriptures to back up his revelation.*

*The first clue was that all of the angels and creatures in Heaven have wings. Then he found multiple references in the poetic literature that spoke of refuge, shelter, and even healing in the wings of the Lord. Finally, Jesus cried out over Jerusalem that He wanted to gather them*

# Worshiping a Chicken

*like a hen gathers her chicks. How had everyone missed this?*

At this point, it should be obvious to the reader that Pete was still suffering the side effects of his overdose. His revelation was extra-biblical and illogical.

It is true that Pete had compiled an impressive list of poetry, figurative speech, and illustrative prophecies that he believed supported his conclusion. It is also true that he believed that these Scriptures implied that God was a chicken. His fervent faith did not make his conclusion correct.

How did Pete end up so far from the truth? He was sincere, but He made several mistakes.

**1.** He searched for passages to validate what he already believed. He did not allow the Bible to speak for itself.

**2.** He accepted a conclusion that is never actually stated. If God wanted us to know that He is a divine fowl, there should be at least one verse among the thousands that clearly defined Him this way.

**3.** He was not familiar enough with the language to understand the figures of speech that he found.

**4.** He built a doctrine on what he thought the text implied. His interpretation violated very clear Scriptures that plainly state that God is an invisible Spirit.

While most doctrines aren't as outlandish as what Pete espoused in our allegory, the truth is that the Bible is misrepresented, misinterpreted, and misapplied more than any other book. How else can you explain the many denominations, theories, and beliefs that exist today?

This does not mean that truth can't be found. In fact, the Bible is the revelation of truth to us. We must skillfully use what God has given us.

# Worshiping a Chicken

**1.** Study the entire Bible.

Too many people have a strong opinion concerning the Bible, but they have never read it all the way through. They read books "about" the Bible, but they haven't read "the Bible." We must diligently read and study all of the Scriptures to fully understand the message.

Psalm 139:17 (NKJV)
"How precious also are Your thoughts to me, O God! How great is the sum of them!"

Instead of simply memorizing a few favorite verses, we must be knowledgeable of the entire Book to ensure that we are interpreting our favorite sections properly.

2 Timothy 2:15 (NKJV)
"Be diligent to present yourself approved to God...rightly dividing the word of truth."

**2.** Pray for understanding.

It is essential that we submit our minds and hearts to the Spirit of God if we want to truly understand the things of God. No amount of study can fully reveal truth without the enlightenment that comes from the Spirit of truth.

1 Corinthians 2:14 (NLT)
"People who aren't spiritual can't receive these truths from God's Spirit. It all sounds foolish to them and they can't understand it, for only those who are spiritual can understand what the Spirit means."

**3.** Believe that the Scriptures are sufficient.

We should not have to add to what God has spoken to discover Him. Let the Bible reveal the Lord and His story. While religious materials, if they accurately present the Scriptures, can be beneficial in helping us to organize, process, and apply doctrines, the Bible is the only book that is essential for salvation.

John 5:39 (NKJV)
"You search the Scriptures…these are they which testify of Me."

**4.** Believe that the Bible is ultimate truth.

The Word is without error. There are not multiple equally valid interpretations. Passages that are difficult can be understood using truth that is more clearly revealed in other verses. We should always try to harmonize any supposed contradictions between Scriptures.

2 Peter 1:20 (NKJV)
"…no prophecy of Scripture is of any private interpretation…"

With these guidelines in mind, what does the Bible really say about God?

**Chapter Two Main Idea: We must be careful to rightly divide the Word and allow the Bible to reveal truth.**

# Just the Facts, Please

## Chapter 3: Just the Facts, Please

**Fact #1:** There is only one God.

James 2:19 (NIV)
"You believe that there is one God. Good! Even the demons believe that and shudder."

Isaiah 46:9 (NLT)
"…For I alone am God! I am God, and there is none like me."

**Fact #2:** God is an invisible Spirit.

John 4:24 (KJV)
"God is a spirit…"

1 Timothy 1:17 (NLT)
"…He is the eternal King, the unseen one who never dies; he alone is God."

1 Timothy 6:15-16 (NIV)
"…God, the blessed and only Ruler, the King of kings and Lord of lords, who alone is

immortal and who lives in unapproachable light, whom no one has seen or can see…"

**Fact #3:** The one God, an invisible Spirit, promised to be our Savior.

Isaiah 43:10-11 (KJV)
"…I am he: before me there was no God formed, neither shall there be after me. I, even I, am the Lord; and beside me there is no savior."

Jude 1:25 (NIV)
"To the only God our Savior be glory, majesty, power and authority…"

**Fact #4:** The one God, Spirit and Savior, was seen in the flesh as Jesus Christ.

1 Timothy 3:16 (NKJV)
"And without controversy great is the mystery of godliness: God was manifested in the flesh…"

2 Corinthians 4:4 (NIV)
"The god of this age has blinded the minds of unbelievers, so that they cannot see the light of the

gospel that displays the glory of Christ, who is the image of God."

John 1:1, 14 (NIV)
"...the Word was God...The Word became flesh."

**Fact #5:** The prophets declared that Jesus is the one God.

Matthew 1:22-23 (KJV)
"Now all this was done, that it might be fulfilled which was spoken by the Lord through the prophet, saying, Behold, the virgin shall be with child, and bear a Son, and they shall call His name Immanuel, which being interpreted is, God with us."

Isaiah 9:6 (NLT)
"For a child is born to us, a son is given to us. The government will rest on his shoulders. And he will be called: Wonderful Counselor, Mighty God, Everlasting Father, Prince of Peace."

**Fact #6:** The apostles declared that Jesus is the one God.

# Just the Facts, Please

John 20:28 (KJV)
"And Thomas answered and said to him, My LORD and my God."

Titus 2:13 (NLT)
"While we look forward with hope to that wonderful day when the glory of our great God and Savior, Jesus Christ, will be revealed."

Romans 9:5 (NLT)
"…Christ himself was an Israelite as far as his human nature is concerned. And he is God, the one who rules over everything and is worthy of eternal praise!"

**Fact #7:** Jesus declared that He is the one Lord God.

Acts 9:5 (NLV)
"Saul answered, 'Who are You Lord?' He said, 'I am Jesus…'"

Revelation 1:7-8 (NLT)
"He comes with the clouds of heaven. And everyone will see him— even those who pierced

him...'I am the Alpha and the Omega—the beginning and the end,' says the Lord God. 'I am the one who is, who always was, and who is still to come—the Almighty One.'"

John 10:25, 30, 33 (NIV)
"Jesus answered...'I and the Father are one.'...'We are not stoning you for any good work,' they replied, 'but for blasphemy, because you, a mere man, claim to be God.'"

**Fact #8:** All the fullness of God dwells in Jesus Christ.

Colossians 1:19 (NLT)
"For God in all his fullness was pleased to live in Christ..."

2 Corinthians 5:19 (NKJV)
"...God was in Christ reconciling the world to Himself..."

Colossians 2:9 (NLT)
"For in Christ lives all the fullness of God in a human body."

**Chapter Three Main Idea: The One God, an invisible Spirit, promised to be our Savior. God was manifested in the flesh. All the fullness of God dwells bodily in Christ.**

# What is in a Name?

## Chapter 4: What is in a Name?

Exodus 6:3 (NLT)
"I appeared to Abraham, to Isaac, and to Jacob as
El-Shaddai—'God Almighty'—but I did not reveal
my name, Yahweh, to them."

God has progressively revealed His name to His
people. Old Testament names for God expressed
His self-existence.

The name "Yahweh," commonly translated in
English as "Jehovah," means "He who is." God
further expressed this concept by calling Himself
the "I AM."

As God would manifest more of Himself,
descriptions were added to describe Him more
completely. Jesus fulfilled all of these descriptions
proving that He is Jehovah, The Great I Am.

# What is in a Name?

**Descriptions of Jehovah - Fulfilled in Christ**

**1.** Jehovah-elyon (Most High) – John 3:31

**2.** Jehovah-jireh (Provider) - John 14:13

**3.** Jehovah-m'kaddesh (Sanctifier) – Hebrews 13:12

**4.** Jehovah-nissi (Victory) - I Cor. 15:57

**5.** Jehovah-raah (Shepherd) – Hebrews 13:20

**6.** Jehovah-rapha (Healer) – James 5:14-15

**7.** Jehovah-sabaoth (Lord of Hosts) - James 5:4-7

**8.** Jehovah-shalom (Peace) – Romans 5:1

**9.** Jehovah-shammah (Present) - Matthew 28:20

**10.** Jehovah-tsidkenu (Righteousness) - I Cor. 1:30

Jesus actually stated that deliverance from sins is only available to those that believe He is the "I Am."

# What is in a Name?

John 8:23-24 (NLT)
"Jesus continued, 'You are from below; I am from above. You belong to this world; I do not. That is why I said that you will die in your sins; for unless you believe that I AM...you will die in your sins.'"

The name "Jesus" is a compound name. It literally translates as "Jehovah our Savior." This name most fully describes God's existence, attributes, and relationship with mankind.

Zechariah 14:9 (NIV)
"...there will be one Lord, and his name the only name."

Matthew 1:21 (NKJV)
"...you shall call His name Jesus, for He will save His people..."

We know Him ultimately as our Savior. The one Lord is now known by one name. The name of Jesus is higher than any other name.

Philippians 2:9-10 (NIV)
"...the name that is above every name, that at the

# What is in a Name?

name of Jesus every knee should bow, in heaven and on earth and under the earth…"

What's in a name? Well, salvation is only in the name of Jesus.

Acts 4:12 (NIV)
"Salvation is found in no one else, for there is no other name under heaven given to mankind by which we must be saved."

**Chapter Four Main Idea: Jesus, Jehovah our Savior, is the name above all others.**

# Yah, Yahweh is Yeshua

## Chapter 5: Yah, Yahweh is Yeshua

The name of God was the great revelation of the Old Testament. God revealed his self-existence through His name. He revealed His attributes through His name. His people were blessed and had His name called over them. They even praised Him by using His name. The great God in Christ would be revealed by the name of God.

Our English word "Jehovah" is an attempt at translating the Hebrew name "YHWH." A better translation is "Yahweh." "Yah" is a shortened or abbreviated form of this Divine name. For the sake of clarity, this is comparable to "Tim" being a shortened form of "Timothy" in English. These are not two different names. They are variations of the same name.

When we say "Hallelujah", we are saying "hallelu" (praise) and "Yah" (YHWH). Praise Yahweh!

# Yah, Yahweh is Yeshua

When we say "Yeshua" (Jesus), we are saying "Yah" (YHWH) and "hoshia" (to save). Yahweh is salvation! Yahweh is the Savior!

Isaiah prophesied about God revealed as the Savior.

Isaiah 12:2 (NLV)
"See, God saves me. I will trust and not be afraid. For the Lord God is my strength and song. And He has become the One Who saves me."

This verse takes on additional meaning when we look at it as it is actually written, without translating the Hebrew names.

"Behold, God is Yeshuwah *(a variant spelling of Yeshua)*, I will trust and not be afraid; 'For Yah, Yehovah, is my strength and song; He also has become Yeshuwah."

"God is Yeshuwah…He has become Yeshuwah." Wow!

# Yah, Yahweh is Yeshua

Here are a few examples to prove that Jesus is Yahweh (Jehovah):

**1.** Yahweh is the first and last. Jesus is also described as the first and last.

Isaiah 44:6 (WEB)
"…Yahweh of Armies says: 'I am the first, and I am the last; and besides me there is no God…'"

Revelation 1:17-18 (NKJV)
"…I am the First and the Last. I am He who lives, and was dead, and behold, I am alive forevermore. Amen."

**2.** Yahweh appeared to Isaiah and told Him that the people would have dull hearts. John wrote that when Isaiah saw Yahweh, He was actually seeing ahead to the coming of the man Christ Jesus.

Isaiah 6:5, 10 (WEB)
"…My eyes have seen the King, Yahweh…shut their eyes; lest they see with their eyes, and hear

with their ears, and understand with their heart, and turn again, and be healed."

John 12:40-41 (NKJV)
"'He has blinded their eyes and hardened their hearts, Lest they should see with their eyes, Lest they should understand with their hearts and turn, So that I should heal them.' These things Isaiah said when he saw His glory and spoke of Him."

**3.** A voice crying in the wilderness would prepare the way of Yahweh (Isaiah 40:3). The messenger would go before Yahweh (Malachi 3:1). John the Baptist fulfilled these prophecies when he prepared the way for Jesus Christ.

Mark 1:2-4 (NKJV)
"As it is written in the Prophets: 'Behold, I send My messenger before Your face, Who will prepare Your way before You.' 'The voice of one crying in the wilderness: Prepare the way of the Lord; Make His paths straight.' John came baptizing in the

wilderness and preaching a baptism of repentance for the remission of sins."

**4.** Yahweh is our Redeemer, yet Jesus redeemed us.

Isaiah 63:16 (WEB)
"…You, Yahweh, are our Father. Our Redeemer from everlasting is Your name."

Galatians 3:13 (NKJV)
"Christ has redeemed us…"

**5.** Yahweh was pierced.

Zechariah 12:8, 10 (WEB)
"In that day Yahweh will defend the inhabitants of Jerusalem…they will look to me whom they have pierced; and they shall mourn for him, as one mourns for his only son, and will grieve."

**6.** Yahweh is the only Savior.

Isaiah 43:3, 11 (WEB)
"I am Yahweh your God, the Holy One of

# Yah, Yahweh is Yeshua

Israel, your Savior...I myself am Yahweh; and besides me there is no savior."

7. Jesus will return just as He left, from the Mount of Olives. In that day, when Yahweh returns to the Mount of Olives, the world will see that there is just one Lord.

Zechariah 14:3-4, 9 (WEB)
"Then Yahweh will go out and fight against those nations...His feet will stand in that day on the Mount of Olives...Yahweh will be King over all the earth. In that day Yahweh will be one, and his name one."

Acts 1:11-12 (NKJV)
"...Jesus, who was taken up from you into heaven, will so come in like manner as you saw Him go into heaven...from the mount called Olivet..."

Our God became our Savior! Yahweh became Yeshua! And He is coming back again!

**Chapter Five Main Idea: Jesus Christ is Yahweh (Jehovah).**

# The One Spirit

## Chapter 6: The One Spirit

I have sought to know the Lord for many years now. I've come to the conclusion that He is beyond comprehension. He is simply too great. This doesn't mean that we aren't responsible to have a relationship with Him. In fact, we are instructed to grow in our knowledge of Him. Like an endless ocean, there is always more to see and experience, and faith requires that we continue exploring and seeking.

Isaiah 40:13, 18, 22, 25, 28 (NIV)
"Who can fathom the Spirit of the Lord...With whom, then, will you compare God? To what image will you liken him?...He sits enthroned above the circle of the earth, and its people are like grasshoppers. He stretches out the heavens like a canopy, and spreads them out like a tent to live in...'To whom will you compare me? Or who is my equal?' says the Holy One. Do you not know? Have you not heard? The Lord is the everlasting God, the Creator of the ends of the

earth. He will not grow tired or weary, and his understanding no one can fathom."

The vastness of God does not justify non-biblical teachings regarding His nature. It is true that we can't articulate the majesty of God properly. We can't put Him in a box and quantify Him so that we completely understand His infinite ways. On the other hand, we aren't given a license to be creative when describing Him. With our limited minds and limited language, it is true that we can't describe Him fully. However, this doesn't justify describing Him incorrectly. He has revealed in His Word what He wants us to know about Him.

Mark 12:29 (NLT)
"Jesus replied, 'The most important commandment is this: Listen, O Israel! The Lord our God is the one and only Lord...'"

The most important lesson of the Bible is that there is only one God. Obviously, this is a doctrine that we don't want to mess up. Later, I will discuss many of the reasons that I reject the Trinitarian description of God, but it all boils down to the Bible emphasizing more than anything else that God is one and never describing Him as three persons.

Jesus is not a person in the Godhead. All the Godhead, the very essence and nature of God, is in Him.

Colossians 2:9 (NKJV)
"For in Him dwells all the fullness of the Godhead bodily..."

God has manifested (revealed Himself) in many different ways. In the Old Testament, He manifested His presence as a fire, a cloud, and a voice. These and other supernatural demonstrations assured the children of Israel that God was with them. Today, He is primarily revealed to us as our Father, in the Son, and by the Holy Spirit.

It is important that we see God as the Bible explains Him. Although He uses various manifestations, in His basic nature, He is a singular, Holy Spirit.

John 4:24 (KJV)
"God is a Spirit…"

Ephesians 4:4 (KJV)
"There is one body, and one Spirit…"

Since there is just one Spirit, we must conclude that there is no distinction between the Holy Spirit, the Spirit of God, and the Spirit of Christ. In fact, Paul actually used these phrases as interchangeable synonyms.

Romans 8:9 (NKJV)
"But you are not in the flesh but in the Spirit, if indeed the Spirit of God dwells in you. Now if anyone does not have the Spirit of Christ, he is not His."

The Bible usually refers to the Spirit of God when describing the invisible presence of God in activity.

# The One Spirit

Genesis 1:2 (KJV)
"...the Spirit of God moved upon the face of the waters."

Numbers 24:2 (KJV)
"...the spirit of God came upon him."

2 Samuel 23:2 (NKJV)
"The Spirit of the Lord spoke..."

Most Christians today also refer to the moving and ministry of God as the work of the Spirit. For instance, it would be rather odd to hear a minister say, "The Son is moving in this service." We would expect to hear, "The Spirit is moving in this service."

In John 14, Jesus made it clear to His disciples that He would go away bodily, but they would continue to experience Him spiritually. Jesus stated that He was "the Truth" (verse 6), that He would ascend to Heaven (verse 2), and that the disciples would receive "the Comforter" (verse 16) to remain with them. He then described the coming Comforter.

# The One Spirit

John 14:17 (NIV)

"...the Spirit of truth. The world cannot accept him, because it neither sees him nor knows him. But you know him, for he lives with you and will be in you."

The Comforter would come, but the world didn't know Him. Who was Jesus speaking of? John 1:10 describes Jesus as the Creator of the world that the world didn't know. The disciples, on the other hand, knew Him and He dwelled with them. There was coming a day when He would dwell in them. Obviously, Jesus couldn't dwell in His disciples in a bodily form. Jesus, the Truth, would ascend, but His disciples would receive the Spirit of Truth. They would receive the Spirit of Christ.

In case there were any questions regarding the true identity of the coming Comforter, Jesus settled the issue in the next verse when He assured them that He would be the one coming to them.

# The One Spirit

John 14:18 (KJV)
"I will not leave you comfortless: I will come to you."

Jesus promised that any time we gather in His name He will be there. He will come to us. How is this possible? The Spirit is not limited by time or space. Because God is a Spirit, people around the world can enjoy His presence and pray with confidence that He hears each of our prayers individually and simultaneously. Jesus is no longer here bodily, but He ministers, comforts, and helps as the one omnipresent Spirit.

2 Corinthians 3:17 (NKJV)
"Now the Lord is the Spirit; and where the Spirit of the Lord is, there is liberty."

Philippians 1:19 (NLT)
"...the Spirit of Jesus Christ helps me..."

**Chapter Six Main Idea: The one Spirit is called the Spirit of God, the Holy Ghost, the Holy Spirit, and the Spirit of Christ.**

# The Father and the Son

## Chapter 7: The Father and the Son

God is our Father. He is the source of life. He created us; therefore, He is the Father of all humanity.

Malachi 2:10 (NKJV)
"Have we not all one Father? Has not one God created us?..."

Interestingly, this Divine fatherhood can also be attributed to Jesus Christ. If we accept Malachi's testimony that God is our Father due to creation, we must conclude that Jesus is the Father because He made all things.

Colossians 1:16-17 (NKJV)
"For by Him *(Jesus)* all things were created that are in heaven and that are on earth, visible and invisible, whether thrones or dominions or principalities or powers. All things were created through Him and for Him. And He is before all things, and in Him all things consist."

# The Father and the Son

There is also a separate father-son relationship that only believers enjoy with our Heavenly Father. In this sense, the righteous are described as the sons of God, while the unrighteous are of their father, the devil.

1 John 3:10 (NKJV)
"In this the children of God and the children of the devil are manifest: Whoever does not practice righteousness is not of God..."

Finally, in a unique way, God is the Father of Christ. Christ is the only begotten Son because He was conceived by the Spirit of God.

Matthew 1:20 (NLT)
"...do not be afraid to take Mary as your wife. For the child within her was conceived by the Holy Spirit."

The terms "Father" and "Son" are not proper names but rather descriptions of a special relationship. The Spirit of God was literally the Father of the Christ.

# The Father and the Son

Matthew 1:18 (NKJV)
"Now the birth of Jesus Christ was as follows:
After His mother Mary was betrothed to Joseph,
before they came together, she was found with
child of the Holy Spirit."

Mary bore the child of the Holy Spirit! In the same
way that Mary was His mother, the Spirit of God
was His Father. Since Jesus was conceived by the
Spirit of God, He is called the Son of God.

However, the Bible declares that He is more than
just the Son of God.

Isaiah 9:6 (NIV)
"For to us a child is born, to us a son is given...he
will be called Wonderful Counselor, Mighty God,
Everlasting Father..."

The Son is also the Everlasting Father, the Mighty
God!

How is this possible? How can the Son also be the
Father? With God, all things are possible!

# The Father and the Son

Here is the key: Jesus Christ is both fully God and fully man. He is both Creator and creation. He is both Father and Son. God chose to dwell in flesh for the purpose of redemption.

2 Corinthians 5:19 (NLT)
"For God was in Christ reconciling the world to himself…"

When Philip asked to see the Father, Jesus identified Himself as being the Father, being the image of the Father, dwelling in the Father, and being indwelled by the Father.

John 14:8-10 (NLT)
"Philip said, 'Lord, show us the Father, and we will be satisfied.' Jesus replied, 'Have I been with you all this time, Philip, and yet you still don't know who I am? *(the Father)* Anyone who has seen me has seen the Father! *(the image of the Father)* So why are you asking me to show him to you? Don't you believe that I am in the Father *(dwelling in the Father)* and the Father is in me? *(the Father dwelling in Him)* The words I speak are not my own, but

# The Father and the Son

my Father who lives in me does his work through me…'"

The only way for this to make sense is to let the Bible define these terms for us.

Luke 1:35 (NKJV)
"…The Holy Spirit will come upon you, and the power of the Highest will overshadow you; therefore, also, that Holy One who is to be born will be called the Son of God."

The one God, an invisible Spirit, moved on Mary. A baby boy, or son, was conceived. Therefore (because of the fact that God moved on Mary), the Holy One would be called the Son of God.

Father: Spirit of God

Son: Child (human yet Divine) that was born.

The terms "Father" and "Son" are distinctions between manifestations but not a distinction of persons.

# The Father and the Son

John 10:30 (NIV)
"I and the Father are one."

John 12:45 (NLT)
"For when you see me, you are seeing the one who sent me."

John 14:7 (NKJV)
"If you had known Me, you would have known My Father also; and from now on you know Him and have seen Him."

1 John 2:22-23 (NKJV)
"Who is a liar but he who denies that Jesus is the Christ? He is antichrist who denies the Father and the Son. Whoever denies the Son does not have the Father either; he who acknowledges the Son has the Father also."

To know and see Jesus Christ was to know and see the Father. To deny Jesus Christ is to deny the Father and the Son. Jesus explained that He is both the source of life (root) and the offspring.

# The Father and the Son

Revelation 22:16 (NIV)
"I, Jesus…am the Root *(Father)* and the Offspring *(Son)*…"

The Son was called Immanuel, which means "God with us." He is the perfect union of God and humanity. Jesus Christ was both limited flesh and all powerful Spirit.

1 Timothy 3:16 (NKJV)
"…God was manifested in the flesh…"

**Chapter Seven Main Idea: The Son was given, born as a child. The Father, the Spirit of God, was manifested in Him.**

# Son of God and Son of Man

## Chapter 8: Son of God and Son of Man

While Christ is the only begotten Son of God, the phrase "son of God" can refer to anyone that is holy and sanctified by God including angels (Job 1:6), believers (John 1:12), those led by the Spirit (Romans 8:14), and saints (Philippians 2:15).

Just as "son of God" describes godliness, "son of man" describes humanity. This expression is used often in the Scriptures. For example, God referred to the prophet as "son of man" over ninety times in the book of Ezekiel.

The Godly nature (Son of God) allowed Christ to live a sin free life. His human nature (Son of Man) allowed Him to pay our penalty for sin and die. Both natures were vital in allowing Him to become our supreme sacrifice. Without the Son (God in flesh), redemption would have been impossible. God, an eternal Spirit, cannot die. He had to become a man to shed blood and lay down His human life.

# Son of God and Son of Man

Acts 20:28 (NLT)
"...God's flock—his church, purchased with his own blood."

Hebrews 2:14 (NIV)
"Since the children have flesh and blood, he too shared in their humanity so that by his death he might break the power of him who holds the power of death—that is, the devil..."

Romans 8:3 (NLT)
"...in that body God declared an end to sin's control over us by giving his Son as a sacrifice for our sins."

**Chapter Eight Main Idea: Both the Divine nature and the human nature were necessary to bring redemption by the Son.**

*Note: In this book, when terms like "human nature" or "flesh" are used, they are used to convey Christ's full and authentic humanity. Another way of referring to Christ's human nature is to simply say "the man, Christ Jesus."*

# One Man, Two Natures

Chapter 9: One Man, Two Natures

Mark Twain wrote the classic story, *The Prince and The Pauper*. The prince, Edward, traded places with a poor child, Tom. Due to their strikingly similar appearances, they each were able to assume the other's role. The prince lived as the commoner. The commoner lived as the prince.

While this is a work of fiction, the concept is easy to apply to reality. If two people look enough alike, identical twins for instance, they could switch roles with one another. There are limitations though. In Twain's story, the prince could not actually be the pauper. He remained the prince. He was simply in the attire of a pauper. Edward could not be Tom, and Tom could not be Edward. It was impossible to be both royal and common at the same time.

The miracle of the Incarnation is a much greater mystery. God was manifested (revealed) in flesh.

# One Man, Two Natures

1 Timothy 3:16 (NKJV)
"And without controversy great is the mystery of godliness: God was manifested in the flesh…"

He did not just have the appearance of flesh, but as we will see, He truly became a man in every way yet remained God.

Philippians 2:6-7 (NIV)
"Who, being in very nature God, did not consider equality with God something to be used to his own advantage; rather, he made himself nothing by taking the very nature of a servant, being made in human likeness."

In His nature, He was God. He was the King of all kings. He chose to take on the additional nature of a servant made in human likeness.

At first it seems impossible. How can one person be both God and man? Maybe an analogy can help demonstrate this concept.

# One Man, Two Natures

Can black be orange? No! Can a triangle be a rectangle? No! Can an octagon be green? Well...actually, that one can be true.

It is illogical to believe that black can be orange. They are mutually exclusive from one another. A triangle can't be a rectangle because their definitions conflict with one another. A three-sided figure can't also be a four-sided figure. However, when we consider green and an octagon, we are looking at two descriptions of entirely different restrictive and exclusive natures. One sets a restriction on the shape (octagon) while the other sets a restriction on the color (green).

We must understand that Deity and humanity are two entirely different natures. His true humanity limits Him to being exclusively one man. His Deity identifies Him as the one and only God, Jehovah. These two natures came together perfectly in Jesus Christ.

**Chapter Nine Main Idea: Jesus Christ is fully God and fully man.**

## Chapter 10: Making a Distinction – Jesus Only

*Brittany, Anne's mom, was worried. What had her daughter gotten herself into? Anne had certainly been raised right. In fact, she had received the Holy Ghost as just a small child. How did it ever get to this point?*

*The trouble started when she got to high school. She started making friends with those "other Pentecostals." Somehow they led Anne into false doctrine. Brittany didn't know exactly what they believed. Pastor Jones seemed disturbed about it all. He told her that Anne was now a "Jesus only" believer.*

*It didn't make sense. How could anyone call themselves Pentecostal and deny the Holy Ghost? And didn't the Scripture warn against denying the Father? Wasn't that the spirit of antichrist? Could Anne even be saved now?*

*Could believing only on Jesus be enough to save someone?*

# Making a Distinction – Jesus Only

It is time to let you and Anne's mom, Brittany, in on a little secret. Oneness believers do believe in the Father, the Son, and the Holy Ghost.

Just for the record, I personally don't have a problem with being called "Jesus only." We are complete in Him because He is the head, God, over all.

Colossians 2:9-10 (NLT)
"For in Christ lives all the fullness of God in a human body. So you also are complete through your union with Christ, who is the head over every ruler and authority."

What we don't like is the implication that anyone who accepts the Oneness view of Christ has somehow denied the Father and therefore isn't saved.

For example, here is how one prominent Pentecostal group, in response to an Oneness revival in their ranks, addressed the issue:

# Making a Distinction – Jesus Only

"Therefore, to deny that the Father is a real and eternal Father, and that the Son is a real and eternal Son, is a denial of the distinction and relationship in the Being of God; a denial of the Father, and the Son; and a displacement of the truth that Jesus Christ is come in the flesh."[2]

The aforementioned organization cited the following passages to validate their statement of faith. (Notice that the Scriptures don't mention anything about God eternally existing as a Son.)

1 John 2:22-23 (NIV)
"Who is the liar? It is whoever denies that Jesus is the Christ. Such a person is the antichrist—denying the Father and the Son. No one who denies the Son has the Father; whoever acknowledges the Son has the Father also."

1 John 4:2-3 (NIV)
"Every spirit that acknowledges that Jesus Christ has come in the flesh is from God, but every spirit that does not acknowledge Jesus is not from God. This is the spirit of the antichrist."

# Making a Distinction – Jesus Only

Ouch!! Did they really use those verses to suggest that anyone that denies that the Son is a separate eternal person of God is a liar and antichrist?

Thankfully, that isn't what the Scriptures say. The Apostle John actually wrote that if you deny that Jesus is the Christ, come in the flesh, then all those bad things are true about you.

These passages were addressing those that claimed to believe in God their Father but didn't want to acknowledge Jesus Christ. If you haven't noticed yet, Oneness believers really, really believe in Christ. No one emphasizes the fact that God was manifested in the flesh more. I don't think anyone can fairly accuse the Oneness movement of denying Christ.

This misconception, that Oneness denies the Father and the Son, is commonly held because so much focus is placed on the Oneness of God that critics often don't realize that there is a distinction made between the Father and the Son. We don't deny that we believe Jesus is the Father. We do, since He is God and is even called the Father, but we can distinguish between His life as a man and His eternal existence as the Spirit.

**Chapter Ten Main Idea: Oneness theology does not deny the Father.**

# Making a Distinction - Mary's Boy

Chapter 11: Making a Distinction – Mary's Boy

Hebrews 2:14-15 (NIV)
"Since the children have flesh and blood, he too shared in their humanity so that by his death he might break the power of him who holds the power of death—that is, the devil."

Jesus Christ was born fully human. He was not God simply in a suit of flesh. He didn't just take on the appearance of a man. He really became a man. If you could somehow remove the nature of God from Him (you can't), you would be left with a common man. He had a human body, mind, emotions, etc. Everything that is present in any other man was also present in Christ except sin. He grew in knowledge and favor. He was hungry. He was thirsty. He was tired. He was sad. He was hurt by His friends. He prayed. He died. He was even tempted by Satan.

To be our Savior, He had to be human. Since a man brought sin and death to the earth, a man had to bring righteousness and life back to the earth.

# Making a Distinction - Mary's Boy

Romans 5:17 (NIV)
"For if, by the trespass of the one man,
death reigned through that one man, how much
more will those who receive God's abundant
provision of grace and of the gift of righteousness
reign in life through the one man, Jesus Christ!"

Jesus Christ restored the relationship between
sinful men and a Holy God. When our sins
separated us from Him, He became Immanuel,
God with us. Jesus Christ was uniquely qualified
to mediate, unite the two parties, because He was
both man and God.

1 Timothy 2:5 (NIV)
"For there is one God and one mediator between
God and mankind, the man Christ Jesus…"

The Son, God manifested in flesh, came into the
world to reconcile us through His death.

Romans 5:10 (NIV)
"…while we were God's enemies, we were
reconciled to him through the death of his Son…"

# Making a Distinction - Mary's Boy

God is never described as actually being a Son until the New Testament. When the Son is mentioned in the Old Testament, the passages are always prophetic, looking ahead to the birth of Christ. The Son is never referred to in either the Old Testament or the New Testament as the Eternal Son of God. Jesus Christ is repeatedly declared to be the only begotten Son of God.

1 John 4:9 (NKJV)
"In this the love of God was manifested toward us, that God has sent His only begotten Son into the world, that we might live through Him."

Begotten alludes to conception or producing offspring. It is the opposite of eternal. The Son was conceived, made of a woman, at a specific time.

Galatians 4:4 (KJV)
"But when the fulness of the time was come, God sent forth his Son, made of a woman..."

A Son must be conceived. God first experienced sonship when He humbled Himself and was born of a virgin.

# Making a Distinction - Mary's Boy

The Son of God is never described in the Bible as a separate eternal person in the Godhead. The Son of God is a man. He is the Christ, the Anointed One. He was conceived by God's Spirit and anointed by God's Spirit. Therefore, "Son" can be used to refer strictly to His humanity. Christ would sometimes use this description to distinguish between His human nature and His Divine nature.

"Son" can also refer to both natures of Christ joined perfectly in the one man, true Divinity and true humanity. God dwells in Him fully. God, while remaining God, took on the nature of a servant. Since the Son is both God and man, the term can be used to distinguish between God existing as the limitless Spirit and God in the flesh.

We can conclude that any time the term "Son" is used in relation to God in the Bible, an aspect of the Incarnation is in view. The passage is speaking, in one way or another, of the man Christ Jesus. In Christ, God placed on Himself the limitations of humanity.

**Chapter Eleven Main Idea: "The Son" is the man Jesus Christ.**

Chapter 12: Making a Distinction – Mary's God

Jesus Christ is God. If you could somehow remove His humanity (you can't), the fullness of God would remain. When God was Incarnate as the Son, He became what He had never been, a man, without losing what He had always been, the Almighty.

**Reasons to believe that Jesus is God:**

**1.** The author of Hebrews referred to the Son as God.

Hebrews 1:8 (NIV)
"But about the Son he says: "Your throne, O God, will last for ever and ever…"

**2.** God is our only Savior, yet Jesus is the Savior.

Hosea 13:4 (NKJV)
"…you shall know no God but Me; For there is no savior besides Me."

# Making a Distinction - Mary's God

Titus 2:13 (NKJV)
"…our great God and Savior Jesus Christ…"

**3.** The Lord is one. Jesus is Lord.

Deuteronomy 6:4 (NKJV)
"Hear, O Israel: The Lord our God, the Lord is one!"

Acts 9:5 (NKJV)
"Then the Lord said, 'I am Jesus…'"

**4.** The Word was God. Jesus is the Word.

John 1:1 (NKJV)
"…the Word was God"

John 1:14 (NKJV)
"And the Word became flesh and dwelt among us…"

**5.** God is the "I AM." Jesus is the "I AM."

Exodus 3:14 (NKJV)
"God said to Moses, 'I AM WHO I AM…'"

John 8:58 (NKJV)
"Jesus said to them, 'Most assuredly, I say to you, before Abraham was, I AM.'"

**6.** God is the King. Jesus is the King of kings.

1 Timothy 1:17 (NKJV)
"Now to the King eternal, immortal, invisible, to God who alone is wise, be honor and glory forever and ever…"

Revelation 17:14 (NKJV)
"…the Lamb will overcome them, for He is Lord of lords and King of kings…"

**Chapter Twelve Main Idea: Although Jesus Christ is the Son of God, He is also God!**

# Manifestation? Oh, I See.

## Chapter 13: Manifestation? Oh, I See.

Philippians 2:8 (KJV)
"And being found in fashion as a man, he humbled himself…"

God willingly chose to experience the world as we do. He humbled himself when He was manifested in the flesh.

Manifestations are limited representations so we can comprehend the limitless God. We could never see all of God because He fills all of heaven, earth, and even hell.

Acts 17:28 (KJV)
"For in him we live, and move, and have our being…"

If God showed Himself fully, everyone and everything would be saturated by His presence.

We find many examples of God manifesting His presence in the Old Testament. Probably the most obvious example is the glory cloud. The Lord was

# Manifestation? Oh, I See.

in the cloud (Ex. 13:21). He came in the cloud (Ex. 19:19). He appeared in the cloud. (Lev. 16:2) His glory appeared in the cloud (Ex. 16:10). It was said that Israel had been face to face with God because His cloud stayed over them. (Numbers 14:14) Exodus 40:38 describes it as "the cloud of Yahweh."

What was the cloud? It was a visible demonstration of God's presence, but it is incorrect to say that God is a cloud because God is far greater than just the cloud that the children of Israel saw.

1 Timothy 3:16 (KJV)
"...God was manifest in the flesh..."

Just as the manifest cloud of God was truly a cloud, the manifest flesh was truly a man. Physical manifestations of the Spirit of God will also have physical limitations. The glory cloud filled a finite amount of space. The manifestation, not God Himself, had this limitation.

# Manifestation? Oh, I See.

In a similar fashion, the manifestation of God in the flesh had limitations that His Spirit does not have. It is proper to identify the man Jesus Christ as God, but God is greater than the limitations of the flesh.

When God was manifested in the cloud, He still filled all of the earth and Heaven. Likewise when God was manifested in the flesh, He still filled all of the earth and Heaven. The limitations of a manifestation have never limited the one God being manifested. The Father was in the Son, yet God was greater than the Son.

John 14:28 (KJV)
"...My Father is greater than I."

**Chapter Thirteen Main Idea: Manifestations of God's presence must have limitations so that we can see and understand Him. As God, He is limitless.**

# The "Man" in Manifestation

## Chapter 14: The "Man" in Manifestation

*Mary loved baby Jesus so much, but He was making things difficult. If Joseph was going to have another son any time soon, Mary was going to have to find some way to get that first boy weaned and potty trained. There was just no way that she could provide that kind of care for two kids and still keep a decent house. Now if she could just convince the miracle child that it was time to grow up a little bit.*

Hebrews 2:17 (NIV)
"He had to be made like them, fully human in every way…"

As a child, Jesus wasn't born with unlimited knowledge. He couldn't read, speak, or walk. He was an infant. As God, He had the ability to do all those things, but He placed limitations on His body.

The limitations of His flesh explain the prayers of Christ. It is overly simplistic to say that He was praying to Himself. As a man, He was overwhelmed by the task ahead of Him. He had all the emotions, stresses, and fears that any other human would have. This is seen in His fervent prayer in the garden. In His distress, He cried out to God.

Hebrews 5:7 (NLT)
"While Jesus was here on earth, he offered prayers and pleadings, with a loud cry and tears, to the one who could rescue him...And God heard his prayers..."

In our spirits, we want to do great things for God, but we often struggle to fulfill these desires because our flesh is weak. Christ also had to battle His flesh. He experienced all the weaknesses that we experience as humans. His flesh had to yield to the will of the Spirit.

Hebrews 4:15 (NIV)
"We do not have a high priest (Jesus) who is unable to empathize with our weaknesses, but we have one who has been tempted in every way, just as we are—yet he did not sin."

# The "Man" in Manifestation

It would not be proper to say that the Father (God) was tempted but rather that the Son (man) was tempted. The flesh cried out to the Spirit. The man cried out to God. The Son prayed to the Father that dwelled in Him.

The limitations of the Son are further demonstrated in a statement recorded in the gospel of Mark.

Mark 13:32 (NIV)
"But about that day or hour no one knows, not even the angels in heaven, nor the Son, but only the Father."

We must accept and try to understand that He was human. He did not come and experience the world solely as God. God did not allow the human mind of Christ to have all knowledge. Jesus, speaking as a man, said that He did not know the day or hour. God, dwelling in Christ, has no such limitation.

# The "Man" in Manifestation

Colossians 2:3 (NLV)
"In Christ are hidden all the riches of wisdom and understanding."

Knowledge does not define a person. Physical appearance does not define a person. As humans, our knowledge and our physical appearances change, but we remain the same persons. It is our spirits and names that distinguish us. Jesus Christ, while limiting Himself physically and mentally, carried the name and the Spirit of the Eternal God.

John 10:30 (KJV)
"I and my Father are one."

Any distinction refers to the distinct natures, God and man, that were joined in Christ and not to the unchanging essence or person of God.

Hebrews 1:3 (KJV)
"Who *(Christ)* being the brightness of his glory, and the express image of his person..."

Jesus is the visible image of the invisible person of God.

# The "Man" in Manifestation

**Chapter Fourteen Main Idea: Any distinction
between the Father and the Son is due to His
manifestation in the flesh.**

# When the King Became the Prince

## Chapter 15: When the King Became the Prince

Revelation 17:14 (KJV)
"...the Lamb...is Lord of lords and King of kings..."

Jesus Christ is the King of all kings. He stated that He has all the power of Heaven and earth (Matthew 28:18). He is described as the only Potentate (1 Timothy 6:15).

Philippians 2:10 (NKJV)
"That at the name of Jesus every knee should bow, of those in heaven, and of those on earth, and of those under the earth..."

How powerful is our King? At the mere mention of His name, everything, including all of Heaven, has to bow. What a Mighty God we serve!

Oddly, in the greatest prophecy foretelling His coming, Jesus is called the Prince of Peace. How did the King become the Prince?

# When the King Became the Prince

Isaiah 9:6 (KJV)
"A child is born...a son is given: and the government shall be upon his shoulders: and his name shall be called...The mighty God, The everlasting Father, The Prince of Peace."

While listing the attributes of our King, He is the Father, the Mighty God, and the government rests totally on Him, the prophet proclaimed that He would secure our peace as the Prince. A prince is the son of a king. The Everlasting Father would be born as a Son to make peace.

Why do we need peace?

There has always been and continues to be trouble between nations, races, and individuals. Also, unbeknownst to most, there is a spiritual battle that rages in all of our lives. Lust wars against our souls and brings forth sin. Sin brings men into captivity, turns us against God, and eventually brings death. Christ came to unite men together as one and to reunite men with God.

# When the King Became the Prince

Colossians 1:15, 19-22 (NLT)
"Christ is the visible image of the invisible
God...For God in all his fullness was pleased to
live in Christ, and through him God reconciled
everything to himself. He made peace with
everything in heaven and on earth by means of
Christ's blood on the cross. This includes you who
were once far away from God. You were his
enemies, separated from him by your evil
thoughts and actions. Yet now he has reconciled
you to himself through the death of Christ in his
physical body. As a result, he has brought you
into his own presence, and you are holy and
blameless as you stand before him without a
single fault."

Only through His death could death be
conquered. Only through His sorrow could we
have peace. The chastisement (punishment) for
our peace was upon Him. He reconciled us in His
body.

What a miracle! What a mystery! The Righteous
One became sin for all so that all sinners could

become righteous. The Immortal took on a mortal body so that mortals could one day take on immortality. The King (Father) brought peace by becoming a Prince (Son).

1 Thessalonians 5:23 (NIV)
"May God himself, the God of peace, sanctify you through and through. May your whole spirit, soul and body be kept blameless at the coming of our Lord Jesus Christ."

Ephesians 2:13-14 (NIV)
"But now in Christ Jesus you who once were far away have been brought near by the blood of Christ. For he himself is our peace…"

**Chapter Fifteen Main Idea: The Almighty God, the King of kings, was born the Prince of peace.**

# A Warm Heart and a Sore Head

## Chapter 16: A Warm Heart and a Sore Head

Many people love God, but they don't understand Him. They like to feel His presence, but the Godhead seems to be beyond their grasps. This is expected in new believers, but we can't stay in ignorance.

2 Peter 3:18 (NLT)
"...you must grow in the grace and knowledge of our Lord and Savior Jesus Christ. All glory to him, both now and forever! Amen."

There is nothing more important than knowing our Savior. False beliefs can lead to false practices, so it is imperative that we grow in our knowledge of God.

If this is all making your head hurt, don't stop reading. Just say a prayer right now for revelation...and a prayer for your headache. God will help you.

So why does it have to be so hard?

# A Warm Heart and a Sore Head

**1.** There is no point of reference. Christ is the "only begotten Son." It has never happened before and will never happen again. The Bible acknowledges the complexity of the Incarnation, but it also plainly declares that Jesus Christ was true humanity and the one God Almighty.

1 Timothy 3:16 (NKJV)
"And without controversy great is the mystery of godliness: God was manifest in the flesh, justified in the Spirit, seen of angels, preached unto the Gentiles, believed on in the world, received up into glory."

**2.** Tradition is a very powerful force and sometimes leads to erroneous ideas. It affects our perceptions. Our assumptions of truth can hinder us from finding truth. The religious missed the first coming of the Messiah because He did not arrive according to their presumptions.

John 1:10 (KJV)
"He was in the world, and the world was made by him, and the world knew him not."

# A Warm Heart and a Sore Head

Many people use the Bible like a drunkard uses a light post. It was given for the purpose of illumination, but it is easy to lean on it only to support your position. We must sincerely study and seek to find truth.

Colossians 2:8-10 (NKJV)
"Beware lest anyone cheat you through philosophy and empty deceit, according to the tradition of men...For in Him dwells all the fullness of the Godhead bodily; and you are complete in Him, who is the head of all principality and power."

3. Jesus was secretive about His true identity. He could have proven His Divinity to the most ardent doubters if that had been His desire. We know there is coming a day when He will show Himself in power and every knee will bow and every tongue will confess, but that was not the purpose of His first coming.

He humbled Himself. He came as a servant instead of as the King. Jesus spoke cryptically so that He would not completely reveal Himself. He hid the truth of who He was so that He could interact man to man with saints and sinners alike.

Consider the following:

**A.** Jesus deflected praise that was offered to Him. It wasn't that He didn't deserve it. It just wasn't yet time to publicly accept it.

Mark 10:18 (NKJV)
"Jesus said to him, 'Why do you call Me good? No one is good but One, that is, God.'"

**B.** Jesus silenced the demons so that they could not reveal His identity.

Mark 1:34 (NIV)
"…he would not let the demons speak because they knew who he was."

**C.** Early in His ministry, He asked recipients of healing not to testify of the great thing that He had done.

# A Warm Heart and a Sore Head

Mark 1:43-44 (NLT)
"Jesus sent him on his way with a stern
warning: 'Don't tell anyone about this…'"

**D.** The disciples were not allowed to reveal their
experience on the Mount of Transfiguration.

Mark 9:9 (NKJV)
"…He commanded them that they should tell no
one the things they had seen, till the Son of Man
had risen from the dead."

**E.** Jesus spoke in parables when discussing the
Father. Even His closest disciples did not
completely understand Him until after the
resurrection.

**Chapter Sixteen Main Idea: The Incarnation can
be difficult to understand due to the uniqueness
of the only begotten Son, false teachings of
tradition, and the cryptic speech of Jesus Christ.**

# The Words of "The Word"

## Chapter 17: The Words of "The Word"

*Sometimes it felt like a dream. Ryan had always been driven, but he had never imagined that his business, Omrinet, would be so successful. What had begun as a start up company in his garage was now a Fortune 500 technology giant.*

*Unfortunately, the company was almost too big. Ryan felt disconnected. He didn't know his employees, and they didn't know him. Recent numbers showed that morale and production were lagging.*

*Ryan knew that he had to get personally involved. He had built this company in his image. Hard work, customer service, and a passion to create were the traits that he had worked so hard to instill in the cultural fabric of Omrinet. For some reason, management was just not able to teach these values to the staff.*

*It was unlike him, but due to the present condition and the outlook for the future of the company he created, Ryan had agreed to be on reality TV. He would be hired on as management and secretly taped for broadcast each day. He was going to be hands on in the day to day operations. He would be able to see how effective he could be in changing the hearts and habits of the employees working for him.*

*He felt that if they got to know him, he would be the example they needed. He would remind them of successes in the company's history. He would talk about the company's founding and founder. He would tell them that he had seen, heard, and knew Mister Ryan. He would explain Mister Ryan's beliefs and desired goals for the company. The only thing that he couldn't do was reveal that he himself was Mister Ryan. That would have to wait until the time was right. That would be the season finale.*

Christ came to reveal the Father to the world, but He did not immediately reveal Himself as the Father. If He would have plainly declared and proven that He was God, He would have never been crucified. It was only by submitting Himself, living as a man, and dying that He could fulfill His purpose.

# The Words of "The Word"

1 Corinthians 2:7-9 (NLT)

"…his plan that was previously hidden, even though he made it for our ultimate glory before the world began. But the rulers of this world have not understood it; if they had, they would not have crucified our glorious Lord. That is what the Scriptures mean when they say, 'No eye has seen, no ear has heard, and no mind has imagined what God has prepared for those who love him.' But it was to us that God revealed these things by his Spirit."

Christ spoke of Himself primarily as a man. He made a distinction between the visible man that everyone could see and the invisible Father that no man could see. It was only by faith, spiritual revelation, and searching the Scriptures that one could gain an understanding that God was actually in Christ.

2 Corinthians 4:3-4 (NKJV)

"But if our gospel be hid, it is hid to them that are lost: In whom the god of this world hath blinded the minds of them which believe not, lest the light of the glorious gospel of Christ, who is the image of God, should shine unto them."

Only those that were led by the Spirit of God and had a true heart would receive this revelation. When Peter declared that Jesus was the Christ, the Son of the Living God, Jesus exclaimed that this knowledge was not given by flesh and blood. Christ, in the flesh, didn't tell Peter who He was. He acknowledged that Peter had received this from the Father (Spirit of God).

The multitudes with hearts far from God could not receive His doctrine. Christ wasn't obligated to explain precious truths to people that wouldn't value them so He spoke in parables that the people couldn't understand.

Matthew 13:10-11, 15 (NIV)
"The disciples came to him and asked, 'Why do you speak to the people in parables?' He replied, 'Because the knowledge of the secrets of the kingdom of heaven has been given to you, but not to them...For this people's heart has become

calloused; they hardly hear with their ears, and they have closed their eyes.'"

His disciples had hearts that were willing to receive the gospel of the kingdom so Christ revealed it to them. However, they were not yet ready to receive the full identity of Christ.

John 16:12 (NKJV)
"I still have many things to say to you, but you cannot bear them now…"

Jesus revealed the mysteries of the kingdom to them through parables, but He hid the mystery of the King in parables.

John 16:25 (WEB)
"I have spoken these things to you in figures of speech *(Greek: parables)*. But the time is coming when I will no more speak to you in figures of speech, but will tell you plainly about the Father."

We see Christ fulfilling this promise just before His ascension. He explained His identity according to the Word.

# The Words of "The Word"

Luke 24:44-45 (NIV)
"He said, 'When I was with you before, I told you that everything written about me in the law of Moses and the prophets and in the Psalms must be fulfilled.' Then he opened their minds so they could understand the Scriptures.'

At the conclusion of His earthly life, Jesus Christ acknowledged that He was God.

Matthew 28:17-18 (KJV)
"When they saw him, they worshipped him: but some doubted. And Jesus came and spake unto them, saying, All power is given unto me in heaven and in earth."

He accepted worship from the disciples that believed His testimony. To the doubters, He declared that He had all power in Heaven and in earth. The disciples received the revelation and understood that He was more than a teacher, more than a prophet, and even more than just the Messiah. All the doubts were gone. If He had all power, even over death, hell, and the grave, He was and is "the only God our Savior."

Jude 1:25 (KJV)
"To the only wise God our Saviour, be glory and majesty, dominion and power, both now and ever. Amen."

**Chapter Seventeen Main Idea: Jesus Christ did not clearly reveal His identity until after the resurrection.**

# Actions Speak as Loudly as Words

## Chapter 18: Actions Speak as Loudly as Words

John 10:38 (NKJV)
"…believe the works, that you may know and believe that the Father is in Me, and I in Him."

The works of Jesus were not coincidental occurrences. They were intentionally designed as a testimony of Him. Those that were looking for the Messiah could identify Him if they would study the Scriptures.

**1.** Jesus taught with the authority of God.

Matthew 7:28-29 (NIV)
"When Jesus had finished saying these things, the crowds were amazed at his teaching, because he taught as one who had authority, and not as their teachers of the law."

He would say "you have heard" before quoting from the Law. He would then introduce a commandment of His own with "but I say to you." Only God could add to His Words.

# Actions Speak as Loudly as Words

**2.** The Lord has command of the stormy winds that raise the waves, yet the winds and sea had to obey Jesus.

Psalm 93:4 (NKJV)
"The LORD *(Yahweh)* on high is mightier than the noise of many waters, Than the mighty waves of the sea."

Psalm 107:25 (NKJV)
"For He commands and raises the stormy wind, Which lifts up the waves of the sea."

Mark 4:39, 41 (NKJV)
"Then He arose and rebuked the wind, and said to the sea, 'Peace, be still!' And the wind ceased and there was a great calm. …And they feared exceedingly and said to one another, 'Who can this be, that even the wind and the sea obey Him!'"

**3.** Job stated that God treads on the sea. Jesus fulfilled this by walking on the water.

Job 9:8 (NKJV)
"He alone…treads on the waves of the sea…"

# Actions Speak as Loudly as Words

Matthew 14:25 (NKJV)
"...Jesus went to them, walking on the sea."

**4.** When John the Baptist asked for confirmation that Jesus was the Messiah, Jesus responded by performing the very miracles Isaiah prophesied that God would come and perform.

Isaiah 35:4-6 (NIV)
"'Be strong, do not fear; your God will come... he will come to save you.' Then will the eyes of the blind be opened and the ears of the deaf unstopped. Then will the lame leap like a deer, and the mute tongue shout for joy."

Luke 7:22 (NLT)
"Then he told John's disciples, 'Go back to John and tell him what you have seen and heard — the blind see, the lame walk, the lepers are cured, the deaf hear, the dead are raised to life, and the Good News is being preached to the poor.'"

**Chapter Eighteen Main Idea: The works of Jesus Christ testified of His power and His identity.**

# The Words of Men

## Chapter 19: The Words of Men

*Chad just didn't get this math stuff at all. Why would he ever need to know how to use fractions anyway? Ms. Parker was talking and drawing some kind of picture on Chad's paper, but Chad was zoning out. All of a sudden, he snapped out of his day dream when he heard Ms. Parker say his name impatiently. "Chad, are you listening? Look at this problem. I drew an illustration to help you understand. If I add one eighth and two eighths, what do I get?" Oh boy, he was on the spot now! He looked at the picture, but it didn't help him at all. Why would his teacher draw that? Ms. Parker asked again, "What do I get? Look at the picture and tell me what I get?" Chad looked at the pizza sliced into eight slices in Ms. Parker's illustration and gave the best answer he could. "I'm not sure why, but it appears that someone will give you a pizza if you can add those fractions."*

Analogies are great. They can help us understand content or ideas that are very difficult otherwise. (I've used a few in this book.) However, when describing God there is no analogy that can really

# The Words of Men

explain Him. Some people try to use a three-leaf clover. Others use an egg. One of the most popular illustrations involves water, ice, and steam. I've even read a Bible study that tried to unlock the mystery of the Incarnation by comparing God to the ingredients in lemonade.

None of these are close. They aren't apples to oranges comparisons. They aren't even apples to orangutans comparisons. If we aren't careful, instead of bring clarity, analogies can bring confusion. You can't use natural things to perfectly explain a supernatural miracle. In fact, you can't explain a miracle at all. Miracles have no rational explanation.

*Glen: Jesus grieved for his dead friend one moment and then raised him up the next. He was tempted by Satan and shortly thereafter forgave others of their sins. He admitted that He didn't know the future date of the second coming, and then He told the Samaritan woman her past and told His disciples their futures. The only answer to these apparent contradictions is the fact that He had both a Divine nature and a human nature.*

# The Words of Men

*Adam: Two natures? How? Glen, I'm just not satisfied with that explanation. I agree it was a miracle, but you are leaving too many questions unanswered. I believe that I can explain it in a more comprehensive way that will answer all the questions. Just give me a little time to think and discuss it with some of my intelligent friends. We will come up with a better explanation.*

Take Adam's response in this scenario; multiply it by thousands of people and hundreds of years. Add a corrupt empire and a backslidden church. You have everything necessary for the birth of false doctrine.

Most people don't realize that the Trinitarian doctrine developed over time. There is no record of any Christians believing anything like the modern position until hundreds of years after the church was founded by Christ.

*The World Book Encyclopedia: "In 325 A.D., in the heat of debate and argument, the Trinitarian theory was first authoritatively set forth, although unexplained and unscriptural."*[3]

# The Words of Men

If it is unscriptural, why do so many people believe it? How did we get to this point? Very slowly, actually.

*The Catholic Encyclopedia: "The Christian dogma of the trinity, only very slowly developed between the 3rd and 8th centuries. It was an attempt to harmonize the various passages, in which the Father, Son, and Holy Ghost are noticed in the New Testament. Only in the last quadrant of the 4th century that what might be called the definitive dogma of the One God in three persons became thoroughly assimilated into Christian life and thought."[4]*

Tertullian (150-225 A.D.) was the first person recorded by history to use the non-biblical phrase, "three persons in one substance" to describe God. His statements, over one hundred years after the death of Christ, are the earliest record that we have of the Latin Church being introduced to the concept of a "Trinity".

This doctrine was not immediately accepted. In fact, Tertullian admitted that most believers rejected his ideas as false. He wrote, "The simple, indeed, who always constitute the majority of believers, are startled at the dispensation, (of the Three in One), on the ground that their very rule of faith withdraws them from the world's plurality of gods to the only true God." [5]

When pressed to explain his faith, he wrote, "It is to be believed because it is absurd." [6] Many today use a similar argument when trying to explain "the mystery" of the Trinity. This argument that we can't truly understand the most basic nature of God effectively eliminates scrutiny of the doctrine, but it violates Scripture.

Romans 1:20 (NKJV)
"For since the creation of the world His invisible attributes are clearly seen…even His eternal power and Godhead, so that they are without excuse…"

Although he is credited by some as being the father of Trinitarian thought, Tertullian would not be considered an orthodox Trinitarian today.

# The Words of Men

When Tertullian spoke of God being three persons, he did not believe that Jesus was an eternal Son. He believed that the Son was God's answer for the sins of creation. The Catholic Encyclopedia states that for Tertullian, "There was a time when there was no Son and no sin, when God was neither Father nor Judge."[7]

The major mistake that Tertullian made was articulating his doctrine outside of the Bible. The Latin "personae" was commonly used to describe a personality or even the mask of a character. The same actor could play multiple parts as long as he changed his "personae."

"Personae" may be a good term for a character changing parts in a production, but it doesn't adequately describe God. He did not play the Father and then play the Son. Simultaneously, He was both Father and Son.

The seeds that Tertullian planted with non-biblical terminology would continue to grow. His terminology was eventually adopted by much of the church. There were centuries of debate concerning the nature of Christ as theologians continued to look further and further outside of the Word to understand God in Christ.

The full doctrine of the Trinity as it is believed today was not formally accepted until 381 A.D. Well over three hundred years after the death of Christ, an unrepentant emperor presided over a church council to develop and articulate this doctrine.

Acceptance of their decision was mandatory. The "personaes" of Tertullian soon were firmly entrenched in Christian doctrine as eternal persons.

*The Encyclopedia Britannica: "After the newly organized Roman Catholic Church was set in order with the decision made by its new head, Constantine, that the Trinity, and the Trinitarian formula only should be used. All who disagreed with this policy were branded as heretics, and many of the leaders were banished, suffering cruel punishments."*[8]

# The Words of Men

**Chapter Nineteen Main Idea: Men have erred by relying on extra-biblical terminology and analogies to understand God instead of relying primarily on the Bible.**

# Who's Report Will You Believe?

Chapter 20: Who's Report Will You Believe?

Finnis Dake: "There are three separate and distinct persons in the Godhead, each one having His own personal spirit body, personal soul, and personal spirit in the sense that each human being, angel, or any other being has his own body, soul and spirit."[9]

Jimmy Swaggart: "You can think of God the Father, God the Son, and God the Holy Ghost as three different persons exactly as you would think of any three other people, their oneness pertaining strictly to their being one in purpose, design, and desire."[10]

Benny Hinn: "God the Father is a person, God the Son is a person, God the Holy Ghost is a person…each one of them is a triune being by Himself…there's nine of them…"[11]

Apostle Paul: "God was manifested in the flesh…God was in Christ...the fullness of the Godhead dwells in Him bodily…God is one."

# Who's Report Will You Believe?

Jesus Christ: "Hear, O Israel; The Lord our God is one Lord...He who has seen me has seen the Father."

**Chapter Twenty Main Idea: There are many different explanations of God, but they don't all agree with the words of the apostles and Christ. You must decide who you believe.**

# A Misplaced Mystery

## Chapter 21: A Misplaced Mystery

*Carson couldn't find his phone. He needed to stop and think. When had he last used that phone? Where had he been when it went missing? If he could remember where and when, he could probably solve the mystery of the missing phone.*

We must acknowledge, as the Scripture does, that there is some mystery in understanding God manifested in the flesh. In fact, Paul wrote that it is a great mystery.

1 Timothy 3:16 (NKJV)
"Without controversy great is the mystery of godliness: God was manifested in the flesh, Justified in the Spirit, Seen by angels, Preached among the Gentiles, Believed on in the world, Received up in glory."

After all of my prayer and study, I still can't say exactly how Christ's human mind interacted with His omniscient mind. I can't explain precisely how His bodily experiences and His omnipresent existence were united.

# A Misplaced Mystery

When trying to comprehend God, it is important to identify where things got complicated. If we can isolate what is actually our mystery, we can follow the correct scriptural path to a resolution.

Israel served God for generations. The nation seemed to have a very clear understanding of God's meaning when He declared, "Oh Israel, the Lord our God, the Lord is One." Why would they not? There is no mention of a Trinity in their Holy Writ. There are, of course, multiple emphatic statements that God is the Holy One that made everything all by Himself. They had many religious controversies through the years, but the definition of "one" was never open to debate. The Lord had made this truth plain to them.

Why do we have the confusion today? When did it start? Jesus is the answer...and the problem in this case.

We all agree that Jesus is God. Isaiah settled this for us when he said that the Son would be called the Mighty God (Isa. 9:6).

# A Misplaced Mystery

When Jesus, a.k.a. God, began to preach and teach, He repeatedly spoke of His Father separately from Himself. In grappling with His words, it was decided over time that God was one, but somehow He was individually God the Father and God the Son. The logic continued, since God doesn't change, He must have eternally existed as Father and Son. Eventually, it was agreed that the Holy Spirit was also addressed distinctly from the Christ so the mystery deepened. God was now believed to actually be three distinct eternal persons with distinct consciousnesses.

There is a problem with this conclusion. Jesus made the exact same distinctions between Himself and God as He made between Himself and the Father. If the unique language used to describe the Incarnation is proof that Jesus is not the Father, we must conclude that He is not God, either. (See table pg. 113.)

If we can believe that Jesus is the Son of God, yet He is God, why is it difficult to believe that Jesus is

# A Misplaced Mystery

the Son of the Father, yet He is the Father? Aren't these two ways of saying the same thing?

| Father | God |
|---|---|
| "The Father has sent me" John 5:36 | "God has sent" John 3:34 |
| "The only begotten of the Father" John 1:14 | "God...gave His only begotten Son" John 3:16 |
| "The Father in me" John 14:10 | "God in Christ" 2 Cor. 5:19 |
| "Many good works I have shown you from my Father." John 10:32 | "Jesus of Nazareth, a Man attested by God to you by miracles, wonders and signs which God did through Him" Acts 2:22 |
| "Father the hour has come...that your Son also may glorify you" John 17:1 | "By what death he would glorify God" John 21:19 |
| "He who has seen me has seen the Father" John 14:9 | "He is the image of the invisible God." Col. 1:15 |
| "The word which you hear is not mine but the Father's." John 14:24 | "He whom God has sent speaks the words of God" John 3:34 |
| "He went away and prayed saying, 'Oh, my Father'" Mark 26:42 | "He...continued all night in prayer to God." Luke 6:12 |
| "The Father raises the dead." John 5:21 | "This Jesus...God has raised up." Acts 2:32 |

# A Misplaced Mystery

The mystery was not in a Godhead of persons from eternity past. The real mystery was in a carpenter that claimed to be the Father visible in the flesh. The Son was not only conceived by the Father, but the Father dwelled in Him fully. Although He could speak from His human consciousness, perspective, and experience distinctly from His Divine consciousness, He was not actually separate from the Spirit any more than we can separate our flesh from our spirits. He is one with the Father.

| Jesus is the Father | |
|---|---|
| The Son is called the everlasting Father. | "A son...his name shall be called...The mighty God, The everlasting Father" Isa. 9:6 |
| God is our Father because He created us. Jesus is our Creator (manifest in the flesh) and thus our Father. | "Have we not all one father? Hath not one God created us?" Mal. 2:10<br><br>"Who is the image of the invisible God...by him were all things created, that are in heaven, and that are in earth." Col. 1:15-16 |

# A Misplaced Mystery

| | |
|---|---|
| Jesus claimed to be the Father because the Father dwelled in Him. | "If you had known Me, you would have known My Father.. He who has seen Me has seen the Father...the Father...dwells in Me." Jn 14:7-10 |
| The Alpha and Omega said that we would be His sons. Jesus is the Alpha and Omega. | "I am Alpha and Omega...I will be his God and he shall be my son." Rev. 21:6-7 <br><br> "Every eye shall see Him, which pierced Him...I am Alpha and Omega...saith the Lord" Rev. 1:7-8 |
| Jesus claimed to be the root (source/Father) and the offspring (descendent/Son). | "I Jesus...am the root and offspring" Rev. 22:16 |
| When we believe the doctrine of Christ, we have both Father and Son. | "He who abides in the doctrine of Christ, he hath both Father and Son" 2 Jn 1:9 |

Consider that both spirit and flesh, though in some way distinct from one another, are essential to our existence. We don't necessarily understand how it works. There is a degree of mystery, but we accept it because we have experienced it and witnessed it to be true. Christ had this same union of the inward man and the outward man as well as an additional union with the fullness of God's Spirit.

Colossians 1:19 (NLT)
"For God in all his fullness was pleased to live in Christ…"

John 3:34 (NLV)
"…God gives Him all of His Spirit."

Jesus spoke and experienced the world as a man, but it was also His prerogative to operate as God. The disciples did not feel obligated to perfectly explain the inter-workings of His humanity with His Divine Spirit. It was enough that they had seen and experienced Him. They were witnesses that the great mystery of godliness, God manifest in the flesh, was true.

As the Son, He dwelled with them, but as the Spirit, He could dwell in them. As a man, He slept on the boat, but as God, He calmed the sea. As a man, He hungered, but as God, He fed five

# A Misplaced Mystery

thousand. As a man, He was confined to the cross, but as God, He filled the universe. As a man, He died, but as God, He was the giver of life.

A misplaced mystery results in seeking answers to the wrong questions. The mystery is in the Incarnation. All the answers are found there.

**Chapter Twenty-One Main Idea: The mystery is not in the singular essence of God. The mystery is the Incarnation.**

## Chapter 22: An Answer With More Questions

*"Since the Bible affirms that Jesus is God, it is often perplexing to note that Jesus addresses God in prayer. The answer to this, as well as to all references to Jesus as being tired or hungry, weeping, lacking knowledge, etc., is that Jesus was a true man, as well as God. The second Person of the Trinity, God the Son, took upon Himself complete humanity, except for our sinful nature, when He was conceived in Mary. He is described by theologians as one Divine Person having two natures, divine and human — the God-man."*[12] - *Billygraham.org*

**1.** Why did Jesus say that His Father was greater than He was?

Trinitarian response: The three persons in the Godhead are actually co-equal even though it doesn't always appear that way. You must understand that Jesus was a true man, as well as God. He was speaking as a man.

# An Answer With More Questions

Oneness response: You must understand that Jesus was true man, as well as God. He was speaking as a man.

**2.** Why did Jesus pray to the Father if He was God?

Trinitarian response: The three persons in the Godhead are actually co-equal even though it doesn't always appear that way. You must understand that Jesus was a true man, as well as God. He was speaking as a man

Oneness response: You must understand that Jesus was a true man, as well as God. He was speaking as a man.

**3.** If Jesus was God and therefore knows everything, why didn't He know the day of His second coming?

Trinitarian response: The three persons in the Godhead are actually co-equal even thought it doesn't always appear that way. You must understand that Jesus was a true man, as well as God. He was speaking as a man.

Oneness response: You must understand that Jesus was a true man, as well as God. He was speaking as a man.

**4.** If Jesus was God, why did He say that you could blaspheme the Son and be forgiven but you wouldn't be forgiven if you blasphemed the Holy Ghost?

Trinitarian response: The three persons in the Godhead are actually co-equal even though it doesn't always appear that way. You must understand that Jesus was a true man, as well as God. He was speaking as a man.

Oneness response: You must understand that Jesus was a true man, as well as God. He was speaking as a man.

These are just a few of the "gotcha" questions that I have been asked when witnessing about the One Mighty God in Christ to my Trinitarian friends.

# An Answer With More Questions

Both Trinitarian and Oneness believers have essentially the same answer. It is the mystery of God Incarnate. The difference is that the Trinitarian answer adds additional doctrine that is never explained in the Old Testament, by Jesus, or by any of His apostles.

Instead of answering difficult questions that do exist, the Trinitarian doctrine so muddies the waters that most Trinitarians don't even realize these questions apply to their belief system. It is all so mysterious, beyond any level of comprehension, that there is no need to seek clarity. Basically, if you accept that three persons with three distinct Divine minds can be just one God, you aren't likely to question specifics. This blind acceptance does not make the questions any less valid when critiquing the Trinitarian belief.

**Chapter Twenty-Two Main Idea: The dual nature of Christ is the only answer to the mysteries of the Incarnation. Jesus Christ was God, but He also spoke, thought, felt, and acted as a man.**

# Choosing the Narrow Way

## Chapter 23: Choosing the Narrow Way

Many people are shocked when they first begin to study the Godhead and to examine things that they have always assumed to be true. They see that the fullness of God dwelling in Christ is plainly explained in the Bible. It makes sense to them. Some will even admit that they feel the Holy Ghost confirming it.

After being convinced of the Oneness of God, they must decide if they will act on it. For some, they have to lay down their pride, reject traditional beliefs, and admit to themselves what they now know to be true. If they are religious, they will also feel pressure from their friends and family. Most people are scared to make spiritual decisions for themselves. How can their new understanding be correct if the people they look up to don't see it the same way?

Some will lose courage. They will go from seeking truth to convincing themselves that the truth they found probably doesn't really matter anyway.

# Choosing the Narrow Way

They may even wish that they had never heard. Ignorance is bliss, after all. Truth is troubling to those that aren't ready to receive it.

Believing is not just an issue of the head. It is primarily an issue of the heart. Everyone comes to the crossroads and must decide if they have the faith necessary to follow the Lord on a narrow path.

This chapter is dedicated to those people hanging in the balance right now trying to convince themselves that remaining in the erroneous traditions of their faith is a viable option. Please consider the following seven reasons why you should not accept the Trinitarian understanding of God.

**1.** The Trinity is never explicitly described in Scripture.

There isn't a text that explains God as three persons. The doctrine is based largely on inferences. This seems odd since the primary purpose of the Word is to teach us about God. The

Bible is, however, emphatic that God is one. Jesus described a belief in the one God and a love for Him as the most important commandment.

Mark 12:29 (KJV)
"Jesus answered him, The first of all commandments is, Hear, O Israel; The Lord our God is one Lord…"

The New Testament writers went into great detail to explain the true meaning of the Old Testament. The significance and symbolism of the Sabbath, the holy days, the priests, the lambs, and the tabernacle are all explained. Paul even took time to teach the proper application of the commandment forbidding muzzling an ox. Yet, nowhere does anyone explain why God, if He really consisted of three distinct persons, so consistently and adamantly insisted that He was God alone, the only Savior, with no one like Him or beside Him, the Holy One. If true, the Trinity would have been the greatest revelation and the most controversial belief of Christianity, but in the early church no one ever discussed, defined, or

explained this doctrine. Slowly over the course
of decades and even centuries, it was pieced
together by later generations.

*The Encyclopedia Britannica: "The trias and trinity
formula was not uniformly used from the beginning,
and up to the third century."*[1]

**2.** The idea of a Trinity is completely foreign to the
Old Testament.

John 4:22 (NLT)
"You Samaritans know very little about the one
you worship, while we Jews know all about him,
for salvation comes through the Jews."

A baby was born of the Holy Spirit thus He
was the Son of God. This was the first mention of
God actually being or having a begotten Son. We
are expected to believe that this is just coincidence,
that the Son was there all along as another person
of God, and that God just kept it secret for His
4,000 years of relationship with men like
Abraham, Isaac, Jacob, Joseph, Moses, David, etc.

*The Encyclopedia of Religion and Ethics: "...the Old Testament could hardly be expected to furnish the doctrine of the 'trinity' if belief in the trinity is grounded upon the belief of the incarnation of God in Christ, and upon the experience of the spiritual redemption. In the New Testament, we do not find the doctrine of the trinity, in anything like its developed form."*[14]

**3.** The terminology lacks rational meaning.

Words have to mean something. How can God exist as three different spirit persons and then be described as one Spirit? What is the difference in one God as three persons and three gods that are in agreement with one another? Why does the Bible designate the Holy Spirit as a spirit if all three persons are Spirit? What about the terms Father and Son? How can the Son be eternal? What would make him a Son if He had no beginning? Why would the Father be in the Son as Jesus claimed? Wouldn't this make the Father and Son united in one instead of eternally distinct?

# Choosing the Narrow Way

*The Ten Epochs of Church History: "To the simplest and most primitive faith, Jesus Christ was simply God, nothing less than God."*[15]

**4.** The terminology can't be used consistently.

Consider the following examples if we consistently applied the Trinitarian understanding of "God" to mean Father, Son, and Holy Ghost.

2 Corinthians 5:19
"God *(Father, Son, and Holy Ghost)* was in Christ…"

1 Timothy 3:16
"God *(Father, Son, and Holy Ghost)* was manifest in the flesh…"

Were the Father and Holy Ghost in Christ? Were the Father and the Holy Ghost manifested in the flesh? Since most Trinitarians would hesitate to affirm these statements, the definition of the term "God" is altered. "God" describes all three persons, unless "God" must only mean "the Father" to support a previously held tenant of the Trinitarian doctrine. This same flawed reasoning has to be used throughout the New Testament to force the Trinity to fit into the text.

*The Hastings Dictionary of the Bible: "The Christian doctrine of God, as existing in three persons, and one substance, is not demonstrable by logic, or by scriptural proofs."*[16]

**5.** If the Trinity consists of three distinct persons, the Bible is full of contradictions.

**A.** Who created the world?

One Father created us (Malachi 2:10). Christ created all things in Heaven and earth (Colossians 1:16). The earth was without form and then the Spirit of God moved (Genesis 1:2).

**B.** Who was the Father of Jesus?

Jesus is the only begotten of the Father (John 1:14). The Son is the everlasting Father (Isaiah 9:6). Mary was found with child of the Holy Ghost (Matthew 1:18).

**C.** Who raised Jesus from the dead?

God the Father raised him from the dead (Galatians 1:1). Jesus claimed that He would raise Himself up after three days (John 2:19). Christ was raised from the dead through the Spirit (Romans 8:11).

**D.** Who gives gifts to the church?

Every good gift comes from the Father (James 1:17). Jesus gave gifts to men (Ephesians 4:8). The Spirit distributes spiritual gifts to the church (1 Corinthians 12:11).

*The Dictionary of Theology: "The New Testament does not in any way speculate on the trinity (the use of the term is introduced later), but reveals the Father through the Son, in the Holy Spirit."*[17]

**6.** The Trinity under close examination creates many problems while doing little to answer the difficult questions regarding the Incarnation.

The doctrine of the Trinity does not clarify the mystery of God manifested in the flesh. It just compounds the mystery by stating that God eternally exists as three persons, yet He is somehow incomprehensibly just one. While these statements are not biblical, they are believed to be implied. These implications are used to interpret direct statements in the Bible that, when taken at face value, are contrary to the doctrine of the Trinity. This is backwards. Concrete statements should be used to determine the validity of perceived implications.

*The Interpreters Dictionary of the Bible: "The word 'trinity' was first coined by Tertullian, and is not a Biblical term."*[18]

**7.** The Trinity can't be described using biblical terms.

A word doesn't have to be in the Bible for it to describe a biblical truth. For example, the English word "rapture" is not in the Bible, but the concept can be easily described by simply quoting from the Scriptures. It can be depicted using nothing but the Book. Contrast this to the accepted dogma of the Trinity.

Trinity: There is one God eternally existing in three persons: God the Father, God the Son, and God the Holy Ghost who are co-equal, co-existent, and co-eternal.

Biblical word or phrase: One God, Eternal, God the Father

Non-biblical word or phrase: Three persons, God the Son, God the Holy Ghost, Co-equal, Co-existent, Co-eternal

Can anyone describe the Trinity without these non - biblical words? If you can't describe it simply by reading from the Bible, there is a good chance the doctrine isn't really in the Bible.

Words affect thoughts, and thoughts affect doctrines. Doctrines affect eternities. We should stick with the clear biblical explanation for the nature of God.

*The Catholic Encyclopedia: In scripture, there is yet, no single term by which the three divine persons are denoted together."*[19]

**Chapter Twenty-Three Main Idea: Consider the evidence of the Scriptures, the logical inconsistencies of the Trinity, and the witness of history. Accept the biblical revelation of the Oneness of God.**

# The Glory, God Revealed

## Chapter 24: The Glory, God Revealed

Galatians 3:20 (KJV)
"…God is one."

However you describe God, He is one. Since God is a Spirit, He is one Spirit. If you choose to describe Him as a Person, He is one Person. If you choose to describe Him as a Being, He is one Being. In His nature or essence, He is one.

Isaiah 43:3, 10, 11 (NKJV)
"For I am the Lord your God, The Holy One of Israel, your Savior…That you may know and believe Me, And understand that I am He. Before Me there was no God formed, Nor shall there be after Me. I, even I, am the Lord, And besides Me there is no savior."

The Holy One wanted His children to understand that He was more than just a provider, more than just a healer, more than just the banner of victory. God was going to reveal Himself as the one and only Savior.

# The Glory, God Revealed

Isaiah 48:9, 11-13, 17 (NKJV)
"For My name's sake…I will not give My glory to another… I am He, I am the First, I am also the Last…Thus says the Lord, your Redeemer, The Holy One of Israel…"

The one God of Israel promised to redeem His children. This glory, this demonstration of God as the Savior, would not belong to another.

Isaiah 52:6, 9-10 (NKJV)
"My people shall know My name. They shall know in that day that I am He who speaks: 'Behold, it is I.'… all the ends of the earth shall see the salvation of our God."

There was coming a more complete revelation of the Lord. God's people would know His name in a special way. The invisible Father would miraculously be seen in swaddling clothes.

Matthew 1:21 (NIV)
"'And she will give birth to a Son, and you are to give him the name Jesus, because He will save His people from their sins.'"

# The Glory, God Revealed

John 1:14 (Young's Literal Translation)
"The Word became flesh, and did tabernacle among us, and we beheld his glory..."

John described the Incarnation as God tabernacled in the flesh. This alluded back to the Old Testament tabernacle that housed the presence of God behind a veil.

Hebrews 10:20 (NKJV)
"...through the veil, that is, His flesh..."

In the new tabernacle, which first laid in a manger in Bethlehem and then walked the streets of Jerusalem, the flesh of Jesus Christ veiled the glory of God.

The unapproachable light of God had to be filtered so that we could see and comprehend Him. Moses beheld God's glory behind the rock. Israel beheld the glory of God shining on Moses' face behind a veil. The world beheld the glory of God in Christ, behind the veil of His flesh.

# The Glory, God Revealed

Hebrews 1:3 (KJV)
"The brightness of His glory and the express image of His person…"

The glory of God, whether the glory cloud in the Old Testament or Jesus Christ in the New Testament, is God revealed.

The Jews couldn't understand how Jesus could say, "Before Abraham was I am." All they saw was the flesh. They knew that He wasn't old enough to have lived before Abraham. They also didn't understand how He could forgive sins. All they saw was the man. They never saw beyond the veil of His flesh. Many people still miss the fullness of glory that dwelled behind that veil.

2 Corinthians 4:6 (NLT)
"For God, who said, 'Let there be light in the darkness,' has made this light shine in our hearts so we could know the glory of God that is seen in the face of Jesus Christ."

# The Glory, God Revealed

From the beginning of time, God has revealed Himself progressively from one glory to another glory. With each experience, mankind received a more complete glimpse of who God is.

The holy men of old always longed for more of God's glory. They wanted to know His name. They wanted to understand His ways.

Matthew 13:17 (NKJV)
"...I say to you that many prophets and righteous men desired to see what you see, and did not see it, and to hear what you hear, and did not hear it."

We are highly privileged to have the life and teachings of Christ preserved for us. We can understand God because of the mighty display of His glory in Christ.

The revelation of God did not cease with His life and His teachings. This was just the beginning. God would prove His love for us through His suffering.

# The Glory, God Revealed

Luke 24:26 (KJV)
"Ought not Christ to have suffered these things, and to enter into His glory?"

Christ entered into His glory by dying on the cross. Now we can perceive the love of God. It is not just some abstract idea or grand claim. His love was demonstrated.

1 John 3:16 (KJV)
"Hereby perceive we the love of God, because he laid down his life for us…"

As glorious as the birth was, as glorious as the death was, as glorious as the resurrection was, there is further glory in the Spirit. The manifestation of the Christ was God dwelling with us. The promise of the Spirit is God dwelling in us.

Receiving the Spirit reveals God in a personal way as He takes residence in our hearts. The veil that hides the glory of God is ultimately removed by the Spirit.

# The Glory, God Revealed

2 Corinthians 3:16-18 (NLT)
"Whenever someone turns to the Lord, the veil is taken away. For the Lord is the Spirit, and wherever the Spirit of the Lord is, there is freedom. So all of us who have had that veil removed can see and reflect the glory of the Lord. And the Lord—who is the Spirit—makes us more and more like him as we are changed into his glorious image."

Colossians 1:27 (NKJV)
"...Christ in you, the hope of glory:"

The Spirit of Christ in us gives us the hope of ultimate glory as we are changed into his image. By the Spirit, this mortal will take on immortality. By the Spirit, this corruptible will take on incorruption.

1 John 3:2 (NIV)
"...we know that when Christ appears, we shall be like him, for we shall see him as he is."

# The Glory, God Revealed

We will see Him as He is, and we will be like Him. We can finally gaze into the light, unfiltered and unveiled. We will behold Him in all of His glory!

Revelation 21:3, 23 (NKJV)
"And I heard a loud voice from heaven saying, 'Behold, the tabernacle of God is with men, and He will dwell with them, and they shall be His people. God Himself will be with them and be their God.'…The city had no need of the sun or of the moon to shine in it, for the glory of God illuminated it. The Lamb is its light."

**Chapter Twenty-Four Main Idea: Jesus Christ is the glory of God revealed. When the process of God's salvation is complete, we will see Him as He really is.**

# Who do You Say I Am?

## Chapter 25: Who do You Say I Am?

Matthew 16:15 (NIV)
"'But what about you?' he asked. 'Who do you say I am?'"

This is my conclusion using the inspired words of the Scriptures as my guide:

There is one Eternal God (1 Timothy 1:17), our Heavenly Father (Malachi 2:10). Jesus said that the Father was in Him (John 10:38). All the fullness of the Godhead dwells in Him bodily (Colossians 2:9). Since God fully dwells in Christ, He is the perfect mediator, both man and God (1 Timothy 2:5). The Son is the Mighty God and Everlasting Father (Isaiah 9:6). Jesus repeated this truth when He explained that He is one with the Father (John 10:30). When you see Him, you see the Father (John 14:9). He is the image of God (2 Corinthians 4:4), manifesting God in the flesh (1 Timothy 3:16). We are complete in Him (Colossians 2:10).

# Who do You Say I Am?

Philippians 2:11 (NKJV)
"Every tongue should confess that Jesus
Christ is Lord, to the glory of God the Father."

**Chapter Twenty-Five Main Idea: When we
confess that Jesus Christ truly is the Lord, God
receives the glory.**

# Introduction to the Appendices

My prayer is that your heart has been opened to the wonderful truth of God in Christ. This book is only an introduction to this great doctrine. I have included the appendices as tools to help you further apply this truth to your Christian walk.

**Application of Oneness Theology:** Appendix A – Appendix C

**Keys to Understanding:** Appendix D

**Answers to Common Questions:** Appendix E

# Appendix A – The Spirit

## The Spirit

Pentecostals are often criticized for an overemphasis on the Holy Ghost. However, our belief in the essentiality of the Spirit in the life of a Christian is the only logical conclusion since we understand that the Holy Ghost is the Spirit of Christ.

We must receive the Holy Ghost, be led of the Holy Ghost, and pray in the Spirit. This is synonymous with receiving Christ and following Him.

1 Corinthians 15:45 (NLT)
"…the last Adam—that is, Christ—is a life-giving Spirit."

2 Corinthians 3:17 (KJV)
"Now the Lord is that Spirit: and where the Spirit of the Lord is, there is liberty."

Romans 8:9 (NIV)
"…if anyone does not have the Spirit of Christ, they do not belong to Christ."

# Appendix A – The Spirit

Because of the vital nature of the Spirit, the disciples waited in fervent anticipation for the promise of the Father until the Holy Ghost was finally poured out on the day of Pentecost.

Acts 2:1, 4 (NKJV)
"When the Day of Pentecost had fully come, they were all with one accord in one place... And they were all filled with the Holy Spirit and began to speak with other tongues, as the Spirit gave them utterance."

Similarly, in the midst of a great revival, Peter and John were sent to Samaria to pray that the Samaritans might receive the Holy Ghost. Healings weren't enough. Deliverances weren't enough. Water baptisms weren't enough. If God's church was going to thrive in Samaria, the saints would have to be filled with the power of the Spirit.

Acts 8:14-17 (NLT)
"When the apostles in Jerusalem heard that the people of Samaria had accepted God's message, they sent Peter and John there. As soon as they

arrived, they prayed for these new believers to receive the Holy Spirit. The Holy Spirit had not yet come upon any of them, for they had only been baptized in the name of the Lord Jesus. Then Peter and John laid their hands upon these believers, and they received the Holy Spirit."

This expectation for all converts to be filled with the Holy Ghost continued throughout the New Testament. Upon meeting disciples of John that confessed to be believers, the great Apostle Paul immediately went to the heart of the matter when he asked, "Have you received the Holy Ghost since you believed?" This question is just as pertinent today. Christ wants to dwell in all of His people.

Acts 19:2, 6 (NLT)
"'Did you receive the Holy Spirit when you believed?' he asked them. 'No,' they replied...when Paul laid his hands on them, the Holy Spirit came on them, and they spoke in other tongues and prophesied."

# Appendix B – Water Baptism

## Water Baptism

Mark 16:16 (NKJV)
"He who believes and is baptized will be saved…"

1 Peter 3:21 (NIV)
"This water symbolizes baptism that now saves you also—not the removal of dirt from the body but the pledge of a clear conscience toward God. It saves you by the resurrection of Jesus Christ."

Galatians 3:27 (NIV)
"All of you who were baptized into Christ have clothed yourselves with Christ."

Water baptism is essential for every believer. We cover our sinful lives with the sinless life of Christ through baptism. Water baptism is an act of faith, believing in Christ for the forgiveness of our sins.

Acts 2:38 (NIV)
"Repent and be baptized, every one of you, in the name of Jesus Christ for the forgiveness of your sins…"

# Appendix B – Water Baptism

Acts 22:16 (NKJV)
"…Arise and be baptized, and wash away your sins, calling on the name of the Lord."

Contrary to most churches today, the apostles baptized in the name of Jesus Christ. Consider the following examples:

Acts 8:12, 16 (NIV)
"But when they believed Philip as he proclaimed the good news of the kingdom of God and the name of Jesus Christ, they were baptized...baptized in the name of the Lord Jesus."

Acts 10:46-48 (NIV)
"Peter said, 'Surely no one can stand in the way of their being baptized with water.'…So he ordered that they be baptized in the name of Jesus Christ."

Acts 19:4-5 (NIV)
"'…He told the people to believe in the one coming after him, that is, in Jesus.' On hearing this, they were baptized in the name of the Lord Jesus."

# Appendix B – Water Baptism

Water baptism is effective because of our faith in Christ, His name, and His gospel. Just as Jesus Christ was buried and rose again, water baptism symbolizes our old lives being buried with Him and God raising us in new life.

Romans 6:3-4 (NIV)
"Don't you know that all of us who were baptized into Christ Jesus were baptized into his death? We were therefore buried with him through baptism into death in order that, just as Christ was raised from the dead through the glory of the Father, we too may live a new life.

# Appendix C – The Great Commission

The Great Commission

Matthew 28:18-19 (NIV)
"Jesus came to them and said, 'All authority in heaven and on earth has been given to me. Therefore go and make disciples of all nations, baptizing them in the name of the Father and of the Son and of the Holy Spirit...'"

Luke 24:45-47 (NKJV)
"And He opened their understanding, that they might comprehend the Scriptures. Then He said to them, 'Thus it is written, and thus it was necessary for the Christ to suffer and to rise from the dead the third day, and that repentance and remission of sins *(water baptism – see Acts 2:38)* should be preached in His name to all nations, beginning at Jerusalem...'"

Jesus opened their understanding to the Scriptures. The Son that was given was the Mighty God and Everlasting Father. He was Jesus, Jehovah the Savior. They had the authority in His

name, the name of the Father, Son, and Holy
Ghost, to baptize for the remission of sins.

The Great Commission was actually given in
response to the doubts of some disciples.

Matthew 28:17 (NKJV)
"...they worshipped him; but some doubted. And
Jesus came and spoke to them, saying, 'All
authority has been given to Me in heaven and on
earth. Go therefore and make disciples of all the
nations, baptizing them in the name of the Father
and of the Son and of the Holy Spirit, teaching
them to observe all things that I have commanded
you; and lo, I am with you always, even to the end
of the age.' Amen."

Jesus assured them that He was all that they
needed. Notice the emphasis on completeness or
fullness in Christ. Since He has ALL power, they
were to teach ALL nations ALL things that he
commanded. He would be with them for ALL
times. They were to baptize in His name because
ALL of God's plan for relationship, redemption,
and sanctification of men was fulfilled in Jesus

# Appendix C – The Great Commission

Christ. He was not only the Son that laid down His life, but He was also the very God that created us and would infill us with His presence.

Paul preached the same message concerning the identity of Christ and the need for baptism in His name.

Colossians 2:9-12 (NKJV)
"For in Him dwells all the fullness of the Godhead bodily; and you are complete in Him, who is the head of all principality and power. In Him you were also circumcised with the circumcision made without hands, by putting off the body of the sins of the flesh, by the circumcision of Christ, buried with Him in baptism, in which you also were raised with Him through faith in the working of God…"

1. The fullness of the Godhead dwells in Christ.
2. He has all power.
3. We put off the sins of our flesh when we are baptized with Christ.

# Appendix C – The Great Commission

The phrase "in the name of the Father, Son, and Holy Ghost" was included in Christ's instructions to the disciples that would perform baptisms. He only used this expression after opening their understanding concerning His identity. He never intended for the apostles to simply repeat His words. They were responsible to fulfill the Lord's command. Apparently, they all left with the same understanding of His commission.

The apostles' obedience to Christ's last instructions is first recorded in Acts 2:38 when Peter stood and gave the command, "Repent and be baptized every one of you in the name of Jesus Christ for the remission of sins."

What – Repent and Be Baptized
Who – Every one of You
How – In the name of Jesus Christ
Why – For the Remission of Sins

This commandment was given to sinners concerning what they should do (Acts 2:37). We are all responsible to obey this command because we all come to God as sinners. In fact, every single recorded baptism in the New Testament church was done exclusively in the name of Jesus Christ. Every sinner that was given instructions on baptism was told to be baptized in the Lord's name. They were all baptized in that one saving name.

Ephesians 4:5 (NKJV)
"one Lord, one faith, one baptism…"

There is only one Lord in whom to have faith and thus only one baptism. If you were given a Bible and told to find the "one baptism," what would your conclusion be? How should you be baptized? Putting tradition aside and just looking at the evidence, what is the biblical method?

The one mention of "the name of the Father, Son, and Holy Ghost" is easily explained. Judging from their actions, it was understood by all of those actually present as referring to the name of Jesus Christ. Have you been baptized in that one name?

# Appendix C – The Great Commission

| Baptism in the name (singular) of the Father, Son, and Holy Ghost | Baptism in the name of the Lord Jesus Christ |
|---|---|
| 1. Matthew 28:19 | 1. Luke 24:47 |
| | 2. Acts 2:38 |
| | 3. Acts 8:12 |
| | 4. Acts 8:16 |
| | 5. Acts 8:35-38 |
| | 6. Acts 10:48 |
| | 7. Acts 19:5 |
| | 8. Acts 22:16 |
| | 9. Romans 6:4 |
| | 10. Galatians 3:27 |
| | 11. Col. 2:8-12 |
| | 12. I Cor.6:11 |

# Appendix D – Keys to Understanding

## Keys to Understanding

**1.** Acknowledge that Christ can speak or be spoken of as a man, as God, or as both God and man.

**A.** Man

Acts 10:38 (NIV)
"…God anointed Jesus of Nazareth with the Holy Spirit and with power…he went around doing good and healing all who were under the power of the devil, because God was with him."

Jesus Christ performed great deeds, not with human power, but by the power of the Holy Spirit. He was a man anointed and empowered by God. As a man, He prayed, obeyed, and loved God. He had a complete human nature. Anything that is true for any other man in relation to God can also be said of Christ.

# Appendix D – Keys to Understanding

**B.** God

John 8:58 (NLT)
"Jesus answered, 'I tell you the truth, before Abraham was even born, I am!'"

Abraham died many years before the Christ child was born. Obviously, this statement had nothing to do with His human nature and everything to do with His Divinity. Any attribute, praise, or work of God is also true for Jesus Christ because He is the one God manifest in the flesh.

**C.** God/Man

John 3:13 (NKJV)
"No one has ascended to heaven but He who came down from heaven, that is, the Son of Man who is in heaven."

Christ spoke as a man on earth while also acknowledging that He was simultaneously the omnipresent God in Heaven. The Son, the child that was given, was the mighty God.

# Appendix D – Keys to Understanding

**2.** Consider the perspective of the audience. Prior to their Christian conversions, much of the original audience reading the epistles had been either radically monotheistic Jews (believers in strictly one God) or Greeks that were followers of the Hebrew faith. They would have seen and understood everything through the perspective of the great revelation of the Old Testament, God is one.

The Trinitarian doctrine was hundreds of years away from being fully formulated, so no one in the first generation would read the apostles' writings with a modern Trinitarian's perspective.

**3.** Consider the perspective of the authors. They either personally knew Him or at least knew of Jesus Christ as a man. Today, we typically understand Jesus primarily as God and struggle to understand His authentic humanity. We see Him as the God who is a man. Their experience was the opposite of ours. They had initially struggled to see Him as God since he was their friend and teacher. Their perspective of Jesus would tend to be of the man who is God.

**4.** Consider the style of the literature. In prophecy, God speaks of future events in the present tense. He calls things that are not (yet) as if they are. For example, in Isaiah 9:6, a child is born though He would not come for many years. Psalms 45:6-7 states that the King reigning in righteousness (Christ) is God and that God has anointed him above His fellows. Before the Incarnation, He had no fellows. It would be many years later before this prophecy came to fruition when Christ was born a man, called us brothers, and redeemed us in the flesh.

Poetry and Prophetic Literature are highly figurative. Generally, the Bible is to be read as it is literally written. However, just like any other book, literary devices can be used. Figures of speech, metaphors, and idiomatic expressions are all used in the Bible.

# Appendix D – Keys to Understanding

This doesn't mean that we each have the authority to decide for ourselves how to interpret and apply a passage. Some believers fall into error by interpreting everything as symbolic. No Scripture was given for private interpretation. The Word has a definite meaning and was given to convey a specific message.

When symbolism is clearly evident, the passage should not be taken as a literal occurrence. For example, Daniel saw a vision that portrayed God as an old man. The same vision portrayed kingdoms as beasts and kings as horns. This vision was symbolic. If nations aren't literally beasts and kings aren't literally horns, why would we believe that God literally exists in Heaven bodily as an old man?

In ancient Israel, the patriarchs (old men) in the family were to be revered and honored. They were esteemed as wise. They also controlled the family's wealth and possessions. They would bless the children both financially and spiritually. In that context, portraying God as "The Ancient of

Days" makes sense. He deserves honor, has all wisdom and power, and blesses His children.

This is just one of many examples that uses imagery to portray the invisible Spirit of God. He is compared to a lion, a flower, and a rock. His presence is described as His face. His power is described as His right hand. He is even said to have wings and feathers. These symbols all emphasized attributes of God in a vivid way.

**5.** Use the Word. The Bible explains the Bible better than any other author ever could. Find other Scriptures that address the same topic to help explain difficult passages. Align your interpretation with the testimony of the entirety of the Book. There will be no contradiction.

# Appendix E – Common Questions

## I. Why did God say, "Let us make man?"

In Hebrew, plurals were used not only to show number (more than one) but also to strengthen the idea of a word. For example, Qadosh (singular) is translated as "holy." Qedoshim (plural) is translated as "most holy."

There is even an example of an earthly ruler using a plural pronoun when speaking about himself. In Ezra 4:18, King Artaxerxes, accentuating His power and position, referred to himself as "us."

Many scholars, both Oneness and Trinitarian, accept the majestic plural as a likely explanation for this verse because of the context. In Genesis 1:26, God emphasized His greatness (let us) as He created man. Verse 27 then explains that God made man in His (singular) own image.

Genesis 1:27 (NKJV)
"God created man in his own image, in the image of God He created him; male and female created he them."

# Appendix E – Common Questions

If God's intention was to highlight His eternal existence in multiple persons, why didn't He consistently refer to Himself using plural pronouns? Throughout the Bible, God is referred to as "He" and never as "They."

There are actually multiple possible explanations for this passage other than God existing as a Trinity that better agree with the full testimony of the Scriptures. Some speculate that God may have been speaking to the angels since other passages record their presence at creation. Others think that He may have been speaking to the dust of the ground that would be used to form man since the Bible occasionally records Him speaking to inanimate objects that He created. It is even possible that God was prophetically speaking ahead to the man Christ Jesus, the first born from the dead, who's resurrected image we will be changed into.

1 Corinthians 15:49-52 (NIV)
"And just as we have borne the image of the earthly man, so shall we bear the image of the

heavenly man...we will all be changed - in a flash, in the twinkling of an eye, at the last trumpet. For the trumpet will sound, the dead will be raised imperishable, and we will be changed."

In any case, we know that the Holy One is our only Creator, Savior, and King.

Isaiah 43:11, 15 (KJV)
"I, even I, am the Lord; and beside me there is no saviour... I am the Lord, your Holy One, the creator...your King."

# Appendix E – Common Questions

## II. Why do the salutations include the Father and the Son?

2 Corinthians 1:2-3 (KJV)
"Grace be to you and peace from God our Father, and from the Lord Jesus Christ. Blessed be God, even the Father of our Lord Jesus Christ, the Father of mercies, and the God of all comfort…"

Greetings similar to this are very common in the New Testament. Isn't it odd that "the Comforter" doesn't send words of comfort? The standard greetings give praise to God the Father and to the Son but don't mention the Spirit, so revealing the Trinity can't be the purpose of these passages.

The words "and" and "even" in the above text are both translations of the same Greek word "kai." The Scriptures show that this is not a distinguishing of persons but rather multiple descriptions of one great God who is our Father and Lord Jesus Christ.

If we take these "kai" passages to refer to persons of God, there would be at least four persons. We would have God, the Father, Jesus Christ, and the Holy Spirit.

1 Thessalonians 3:11 (KJV)
"Now God himself and our Father, and our Lord Jesus Christ, direct our way unto you."

Colossians 2:2 (KJV)
"...the mystery of God, and of the Father, and of Christ."

To make matters worse, if we understood "and" or "even" to always distinguish persons we would also have two devils.

Revelation 20:2 (KJV)
"...that old serpent, which is the Devil, and Satan..."

These verses need to be understood in the style in which they were written. Multiple titles or descriptions were used to add emphasis to the person being described. God was being praised for who He was and what He had done.

# Appendix E – Common Questions

The apostles also had extra motivation to acknowledge the various manifestations of God. The early church was influenced heavily by monotheistic Jews. These Jews believed in Jehovah. Many did not accept that Jesus was Emmanuel, God with us. They desired to worship the Heavenly Father, but they did not believe that the Father dwelled in the Son.

Believing in the Son distinguished the Christians from the other monotheistic non-Christians.

1 John 2:23 (NKJV)
"Whoever denies the Son does not have the Father either; he who acknowledges the Son has the Father also."

The Son is the revelation of God in the flesh. This truth was emphasized and repeated in the introductions to the epistles.

# Appendix E – Common Questions

## III. Why was the Word with God?

Many people read John 1:1 with a Trinitarian bias. They understand it as:

"In the beginning was the Word *(God the Son)*, and the Word *(God the Son)* was with God *(God the Father)*, and the Word *(God the Son)* was God *(God the Son)*."

Word = God the Son
God (first mention) = God the Father
God (second mention) = God the Son

If this interpretation is correct, in a single verse "God" refers to God the Father, though the Father is not mentioned, and immediately after refers to God the Son, though the Son is not mentioned. Also, in this passage, the term "God" would only refer to a person in the Godhead but never to the fullness of God.

The only way to arrive at this conclusion is to read this gospel already convinced that God is a Trinity. It should not require such twisting of the

# Appendix E – Common Questions

Scriptures to discover the author's intended meaning.

If we accept that "God" refers to the Father, the Son, and the Holy Ghost, this first chapter of John summarizes the Oneness doctrine. God, in all His fullness, was made flesh.

John 1:1,14 (NKJV)
"…the Word was God *(Father, Son, and Holy Ghost)*… And the Word *(God: Father, Son, and Holy Ghost)* was made flesh."

The Greek word "logos" is translated into English as "Word." Heraclitus, a Greek philosopher, first used the term "logos" around 600 B.C. to designate the Divine reason or plan which coordinates a changing universe. "Logos" can refer to a thought in the mind or the expression of a thought or plan. According to John, the Word, God's Divine plan, was with Him from the beginning.

# Appendix E – Common Questions

John 1:1 (KJV)
"In the beginning was the Word, and the Word was with God, and the Word was God…"

John did not claim that the "Word" was eternal. Eternity is continuous in both directions with no beginning or ending. The beginning he mentioned must be the beginning that Genesis 1:1 speaks of, the creation of the world when time as we know it began.

From the beginning, the very creation of the world, God had a plan. However, this did not involve another; this Word was God. This Word (God) became flesh. The creative Word or expression of salvation was God Himself. He was going to take on human nature and save the world. God would gloriously reveal Himself as the answer to sin. This was the preexisting glory that Jesus Christ had from the foundation of the world (John 17:5). It was the preordained cross.

# Appendix E – Common Questions

Luke 24:26 (NKJV)
"Ought not Christ to have suffered these things, and to enter into his glory?"

Revelation 13:8 (NIV)
"...the Lamb who was slain from the creation of the world."

Before the world began, in the mind of God, the crucifixion was already a fact. Before man's first sin, God already had a solution so we could be holy and blameless. His "logos" (plan) was to come in flesh Himself, die as our sacrificial lamb, and demonstrate His love for us.

Ephesians 1:4 (NLT)
"Even before he made the world, God loved us and chose us in Christ to be holy and without fault in his eyes."

# Appendix E – Common Questions

IV. Does the baptism of Christ prove the Trinity?

One of the events that is often used to defend the doctrine of the Trinity is the baptism of Jesus.

"It is so obvious. All three of them are present. How could anyone not see it?"

The question is, three of what? Is there really any evidence that there were three persons of God present? Would we arrive at this conclusion by simply reading this baptism account?

John 1:32-34 (NLT)
"John testified, 'I saw the Holy Spirit descending like a dove from heaven and resting upon him. I didn't know he was the one, but when God sent me to baptize with water, he told me, 'The one on whom you see the Spirit descend and rest is the one who will baptize with the Holy Spirit.' I saw this happen to Jesus, so I testify that he is the Chosen One of God.'"

The true purpose of the miraculous signs was not to introduce a Trinity but rather as confirmation that the Messiah had arrived.

Matthew 3:17 (NKJV)
"A voice came from heaven, saying, 'This is my beloved Son, in whom I am well pleased.'"

John the Baptist was looking for one that would baptize with the fire of the Spirit. He was looking for one that would be greater than any other preacher or prophet. Surely John was very familiar with Isaiah's prophecy that the Son would be the Mighty God and the Everlasting Father. The voice and the dove confirmed the same message that Jesus was the Christ.

There were clearly three manifestations of God: the man, the dove, and the voice. This does not prove that there is an eternal God the Father, an eternal God the Son, and an eternal God the Holy Ghost encompassing one God in three separate yet equal persons.

# Appendix E – Common Questions

Would any Jew present that day have left convinced that the one God was somehow three persons because a voice spoke and the Spirit manifested as a dove? God had revealed Himself in a variety of ways throughout their nation's history. If the purpose of this occurrence was to introduce a Trinity, why was it never explained?

The onlookers probably all left believing that Jesus was clearly called and anointed by God. His public ministry was successfully launched. It would not be until His last days, after He had performed many confirming works, that Jesus would clearly articulate His identity to His closest followers.

This event proves that Jesus made a dramatic entrance onto the public stage. It does not prove the existence of a Godhead that consists of multiple persons.

# Appendix E – Common Questions

## V. What about the cry from the cross?

John 8:28-29 (NKJV)
"Jesus said to them, 'When you lift up the Son of Man, then you will know that I am He... He who sent Me is with Me. The Father has not left Me alone.'"

When He was lifted up on the cross, they would know that the Father hadn't left Him. When Christ paid the wage of sin (death), God dwelled in Him.

2 Corinthians 5:19 (NKJV)
"...God was in Christ, reconciling the world unto himself, not imputing their trespasses to them..."

If God was still united perfectly with Christ, what did Jesus mean when He said, "My God, My God, why hast thou forsaken me?"

He was for the first time feeling the weight of sin. Sin separates us from God. As a man, He would have felt like a Godforsaken sinner. The Scripture actually says that He became sin for us.

# Appendix E – Common Questions

2 Corinthians 5:21 (NIV)
"God made him who had no sin to be sin  for us, so that in him we might become the righteousness of God."

Jesus also was pointing the crowd's attention to a prophecy being fulfilled in their midst. David in his psalms would often express His sorrows and need for God's intervention. In the middle of a personal psalm of distress, he would prophetically begin to express the distress of the suffering Savior that would come after him. An example of this is found in Psalm 22.

Psalm 22:1, 14-18 (NLT)
"My God, my God, why have you abandoned me?...My life is poured out like water, and all my bones are out of joint. My heart is like wax, melting within me. My strength has dried up like sun baked clay. My tongue sticks to the roof of my mouth. You have laid me in the dust and left me for dead. My enemies surround me like a pack of dogs; an evil gang closes in on me. They have pierced my hands and feet. I can count all my

bones. My enemies stare at me and gloat. They divide my garments among themselves and throw dice for my clothing."

It is often difficult to know within a Messianic psalm when David was speaking of himself, when he was expressing the feelings of Christ, or when his writings applied to both his current circumstances as well as a future fulfillment in Christ. We can be certain that just as God had not actually forsaken David when he first penned the words, God had not actually forsaken Christ when He quoted the same words in His time of agony.

Deuteronomy 4:31 (NKJV)
"(for the LORD your God *is* a merciful God), He will not forsake you…"

The Trinitarian view of God is just as difficult to reconcile with the cry on the cross. Jesus never said that "the Father" forsook him. He said, "My God, why have you forsaken me?" If Jesus was speaking as God the Son, how could God forsake

# Appendix E – Common Questions

Him? It must have been the man, the Son of God, crying out as He submitted to the plan of God and felt the shame and agony of the curse of sin.

# Appendix E – Common Questions

## VI. What did Stephen see in Heaven?

Acts 7:55-56 (NKJV)
"But he, being full of the Holy Spirit, gazed into heaven and saw the glory of God, and Jesus standing at the right hand of God, and said, 'Look! I see the heavens opened and the Son of Man standing at the right hand of God!'"

Did Stephen see Jesus standing to the right side of God? There are some obvious contradictions if we try to interpret this literally.

**A.** God is an invisible Spirit, and no one can see Him in His Heavenly splendor.

1 Timothy 6:16 (NIV)
"Who alone is immortal and who lives in unapproachable light, whom no one has seen or can see…"

**B.** God is omnipresent. He fills everything and is not limited to one location. Can anyone possibly stand to the right of everywhere?

# Appendix E – Common Questions

Jeremiah 23:24 (NKJV)
"'...Do I not fill heaven and earth?' says the Lord."

**C.** Stephen saw Jesus standing "on the right hand of God." Jesus is God. Can Jesus stand to the right of Himself?

**D.** The Greek text actually uses the plural "rights."

Since the description can't be literal, the "right hand" or "rights" must be a figurative expression. Not only is it used figuratively in this verse, this phrase is used throughout the Bible to describe God's power rather than a location. The "right hand of God" is similar to the expression "right hand man" that is common today. Anyone operating in the power or authority of the Spirit of God was experiencing His "right hand."

We find proof that this expression was used figuratively to describe the glory of the resurrected Christ in the New Testament.

# Appendix E – Common Questions

Hebrews 1:13 (NIV)
"To which of the angels did God ever say, 'Sit at my right hand until I make your enemies a footstool for your feet?'"

If Jesus is literally sitting on the right hand, are his feet literally on top of his enemies?

The New Testament authors and audience would have been familiar with the symbolism of the "right hand" because of its use in the Old Testament.

Exodus 15:6 (NKJV)
"Your right hand, O LORD, has become glorious in power: Your right hand, O LORD, has dashed the enemy in pieces."

Did a huge right hand fall from the sky and crush the enemy, or was this describing God destroying the enemy with His glorious power?

# Appendix E – Common Questions

Psalm 48:10 (NIV)

"Like your name, O God, your praise reaches to the ends of the earth; your right hand is filled with righteousness."

Is this more likely to be describing the righteousness of God's power, or has God found a way to literally fill his hand with an abstract idea like righteousness?

Matthew 26:64 (WEB)

"I say to you, after this you will see the Son of Man sitting at the right hand of power, and coming on the clouds of the sky."

We don't have to guess what the appropriate interpretation is. Jesus explained it for us. The Son of man is sitting on the "right hand of power." If the "right hand" is a physical place, Jesus would need to be standing there (Acts 7:55-56) and sitting there simultaneously (Acts 2:34). Also, at the second coming, He would be sitting at the right hand and coming in the clouds simultaneously (Matthew 26:64).

# Appendix E – Common Questions

What did Stephen actually see? The passage never states that Stephen saw the Spirit of God. It says that he saw "the glory of God." What is the glory of God?

Hebrews 1:3 (KJV)
"Who being the brightness of his glory, and the express image of his person, and upholding all things by the word of his power, when he had by himself purged our sins, sat down on the right hand of the Majesty on high..."

Jesus Christ is the glory of God. He is God demonstrated to us. The invisible Spirit is seen visibly in the man Jesus Christ. The only way to see the Father is in the bodily form of Jesus Christ.

Stephen saw Jesus, but He was different than when He was last seen on earth. While He was here, He veiled His glory and humbled Himself, but now that He has risen, He supersedes all authority and powers on earth and in Heaven.

# Appendix E – Common Questions

Similarly, when John saw Jesus in the first chapter of Revelation, he described Him as "like the Son of Man." He was still in bodily form. He looked like the man that John had known, but He was now radiating with power. He was white like snow, His eyes were like fire, His voice sounded like many waters, and His face shined like the sun.

Jesus Christ is no longer experienced as just a humble teacher. He has ascended into Heaven, demonstrating all power (God's right hand), and proclaiming His full Deity as the King of kings and Lord of lords.

Revelation 19:12-16 (NIV)
"His eyes are like blazing fire, and on his head are many crowns… On his robe and on his thigh he has this name written: KING OF KINGS AND LORD OF LORDS."

The book of Ephesians further explains Christ's ascension to the right hand as well as its significance for believers.

# Appendix E – Common Questions

Ephesians 1:19-20 (NKJV)
"…the exceeding greatness of His power toward us who believe, according to the working of His mighty power which He worked in Christ when He raised Him from the dead and seated Him at His right hand in the heavenly places… and raised us up together, and made us sit together in the heavenly places…"

The exceeding greatness of God's mighty power, His right hand, was revealed when Christ was raised from the dead. Because of Christ, we also have the opportunity to figuratively "sit together in heavenly places" at the right hand, filled with the power of His Spirit.

# Appendix E – Common Questions

VII. Why does Jesus Christ intercede for us?

Intercede: *from Latin intercedere - from inter "between" + cedere "go"*
1) To act in behalf of someone in difficulty or trouble
2) To attempt to reconcile differences between two people or groups; mediate
Synonyms: intervene, plead, advocate, reconcile

1 Samuel 2:25 (NLT)
"If someone sins against another person, God can mediate for the guilty party. But if someone sins against the Lord, who can intercede?"

Sin separates us from God. All men have sinned so no one remains to intercede on our behalf and bring us back into relationship with the Lord. Without a mediator, we are enemies of God.

Job 16:21 (NLT)
"I need someone to mediate between God and me, as a person mediates between friends."

# Appendix E – Common Questions

Even the righteous (by our standards) Job recognized that he needed someone to mediate between him and a holy God. What truly righteous man could be a friend of sinners and appeal to God on the sinners' behalf?

Isaiah 59:16, 20 (NKJV)
"He saw that there was no man, And wondered that there was no intercessor; Therefore His own arm brought salvation…The Redeemer will come…"

The Lord must bring salvation Himself. He must be the Intercessor and the Redeemer.

1 Timothy 2:3-5 (NLT)
"…God our Savior, who wants everyone to be saved…There is one God and one Mediator who can reconcile God and humanity — the man Christ Jesus."

# Appendix E – Common Questions

The one God became our Savior when He, in the man Christ Jesus, restored us back to Himself.

2 Corinthians 5:19 (NKJV)
"…God was in Christ reconciling the world to Himself, not imputing their trespasses to them…"

The certain judgment of God awaits everyone with sins still counting against them. Because the penalty for breaking God's law is death, Satan, through temptation, consumes the lives of sinners. The Bible describes God as the Judge, the devil as the accuser (think prosecutor), and the whole world as guilty.

Fortunately, we don't have to stand trial by ourselves.

1 John 2:1 (NIV)
"I write this to you so that you will not sin. But if anybody does sin, we have an advocate with the Father—Jesus Christ, the Righteous One."

# Appendix E – Common Questions

We don't stand before God with just our own works. No one could be saved that way. The man Christ Jesus stands in God's presence for us.

Hebrews 9:24-26 (NIV)
"For Christ...entered heaven itself, now to appear for us in God's presence...he has appeared once for all at the culmination of the ages to do away with sin by the sacrifice of himself."

Through the sacrifice of Himself, Jesus took the record that was against us and nailed it to the cross.

Colossians 2:14 (NIV)
"...having canceled the charge of our legal indebtedness, which stood against us and condemned us; he has taken it away, nailing it to the cross."

All the evidence against us was destroyed on the cross. We deserve judgment, yet He intercedes and offers mercy. We would face certain destruction, but He intercedes and offers salvation.

Romans 8:31-35 (NIV)
"…If God is for us, who can be against us? …Who will bring any charge against those whom God has chosen? It is God who justifies. Who then is the one who condemns? No one. Christ Jesus who died—more than that, who was raised to life—is at the right hand of God and is also interceding for us. Who shall separate us from the love of Christ?"

Christ justified us on Calvary. He forgives us. He leads us. He empowers us. He loves us. There is no condemnation in Christ. He died, was buried, and then rose in the power of God (at the right hand) victorious over the devil.

Hebrews 2:14 (NIV)
"Since the children have flesh and blood, he too shared in their humanity so that by his death he might break the power of him who holds the power of death—that is, the devil…"

# Appendix E – Common Questions

Who can condemn us? Who can bring a charge against us? The devil no longer has any accusation to make. The full penalty for sin was placed on Christ to fulfill the Law. The only witness left to speak is His blood.

Hebrews 12:24 (NLT)
"You have come to Jesus, the one who mediates the new covenant between God and people, and to the sprinkled blood, which speaks of forgiveness…"

The blood speaks forgiveness!

A foreshadowing of the intercession of Christ was seen in the priests of the Old Testament. The priests were ordinary men, yet they were holy and set apart. They would offer blood sacrifices to God for the people. This was an act of intercession on behalf of their Israeli brothers. The priests weren't perfect and the sacrifices weren't sufficient, but they were used to point ahead to the work of

# Appendix E – Common Questions

Christ. He would become like us and intercede for us by offering up His life as the sacrifice.

Hebrews 2:17-18 (NIV)
"For this reason he had to be made like them, fully human in every way, in order that he might become a merciful and faithful high priest in service to God, and that he might make atonement for the sins of the people. Because he himself suffered when he was tempted, he is able to help those who are being tempted."

Hebrews 4:15-16 (NLT)
"So then we have a great High Priest who has entered heaven, Jesus the Son of God, let us hold firmly to what we believe. This High Priest of ours understands our weaknesses, for he faced all of the same testings we do, yet he did not sin. So let us come boldly to the throne of our gracious God. There we will receive his mercy, and we will find grace to help us when we need it most."

# Appendix E – Common Questions

Our Intercessor, the true High Priest, is unlike any that have come before Him. He was a man in every way, but unlike all the other men, He never sinned. He understands our weaknesses. He understands temptation. He offers grace, mercy, and help when we need it the most. He knows how to deliver us from temptation. He knows how to overcome. He died once, yet He lives forevermore. The one on our side is the Victor, and we can share in His victory.

Hebrews 7:25-27 (NIV)
"Therefore he is able to save completely those who come to God through him, because he always lives to intercede for them. Such a high priest truly meets our need—one who is holy, blameless, pure, set apart from sinners, exalted above the heavens…He sacrificed for their sins once for all when he offered himself."

God's desire is for us to be saved. Even when we have sinned, He is still reaching for us. Because of our great High Priest and His blood that He offered up in our place, we can approach God boldly. There is no reason to remain condemned. No one is ever good enough on their own; this is why we needed a mediator. Applying His blood takes away our guilt and our feelings of shame.

1 John 3:20-21 (NLT)
"Even if we feel guilty, God is greater than our feelings, and he knows everything. Dear friends, if we don't feel guilty, we can come to God with bold confidence."

He is offering to intercede and help us. He is the Judge, but He is also the Advocate, the Priest, and the Lamb. He is the compassionate man Christ Jesus and the great merciful God our Savior. He intercedes on behalf of sinners so that we can be restored to Him and saved for eternity.

Romans 5:1-10 (NLT)
"Therefore, since we have been made right in God's sight…we have peace with God because of what Jesus Christ our Lord has done for us…

# Appendix E – Common Questions

Christ has brought us into this place of undeserved privilege where we now stand...we were utterly helpless, Christ came at just the right time and died for us sinners...our friendship with God was restored by the death of his Son while we were still his enemies, we will certainly be saved through the life of his Son."

# Recommended Resources

If you would like to read additional articles from the author concerning the Oneness of God and other Apostolic doctrines, visit **apostolicallyspeaking.com**.

For a more comprehensive study of Oneness, "The Oneness of God" and "The Oneness View of Jesus Christ" by David Bernard are excellent books. "I Am" by David Norris is recommended for those interested in an academic book.

# Bibliography

1. This is a paraphrase of a statement that Dr. Johnny James made in a sermon.

2. "Our 16 Fundamental Truths." *Fundamental Truths (Full Statement)*. N.p., n.d. Web. 24 July 2015.

3. The World Book Encyclopedia: Volume 16, page 7270

4. Tertullian, *Against Praxeas 3*

5. Tertullian, *On the Flesh of Christ*

6. The Catholic Encyclopedia: 1967 edition, volume 14, page 295

7. "Tertullian." *Catholic Online*. N.p., n.d. Web

8. The Encyclopedia Britannica: 11th edition, volume 3, page 366

9. DARB (New Testament), 280, GPFM, 65, 498

# Bibliography

10. Jimmy Swaggart, "Brother Swaggart, Here's My Question", *The Evangelist,* July 1983, 15

11. Benny Hinn, Praise The Lord, TBN October 3, 1990

12. "If Jesus Is God, Why Does the Bible Talk about Him Praying to God?" *Billy Graham Evangelistic Association*. BGEA Staff, 01 June 2004. Web. 09 Jan. 2016.

13. The Encyclopedia Britannica: Volume 3, page 365-366

14. The Encyclopedia of Religion and Ethics: 1951 edition, volume 12, page 458

15. The Ten Epochs of Church History: Volume 3, the Ecumenical Councils page 72

16. The Hastings Dictionary of the Bible: 1963 edition, page 1015

# Bibliography

17. The Dictionary of Theology: 1965 edition, page 447

18. The Interpreters Dictionary of the Bible: 1962 edition, volume 4, page 711

19. The Catholic Encyclopedia: 1912 edition, volume 15, page 4

# About the Author

Landon Davis is the pastor of Marianna First United Pentecostal Church. For more information about the church, visit **mariannaupc.com**.

54624636R00111

Made in the USA
Columbia, SC
03 April 2019